THE AGE OF MYTH

Tom Chetwynd was educated by Benedictine monks and later went on to study Theology at London University. He has been investigating the roots of the major religions in the Age of Myth for the past 30 years and is also author of several books on the unconscious. He and his French wife, Hélène, have three daughters and two grandsons. He is an ardent Catholic, but also practises Zen.

Jack O'Connell
Ashland
28 September 1991

THE AGE
OF MYTH

The Bronze Age as the
Cradle of the Unconscious

TOM CHETWYND

Mandala
An Imprint of HarperCollins*Publishers*

Mandala
An Imprint of Grafton Books
A Division of HarperCollins*Publishers*
77-85 Fulham Palace Road,
Hammersmith, London W6 8JB

Published by Mandala 1991
1 3 5 7 9 10 8 6 4 2

A CIP catalogue record for this book
is available from the British Library

ISBN 0–04–440588–X

Printed in Great Britain by
CollinsManufacturing, Glasgow

CONTENTS

To the memory of

Randolph
Pierre
and all of the forefathers

ACKNOWLEDGEMENTS

First I would like to thank all those experts upon whom my work has been so dependent. I would like to mention especially George Aaron Barton, Wallis Budge, Adolph Erman, Kathleen Kenyon, John Gray, Van Seters and many others, some of whom have been mentioned in the bibliography at the back of this book. Their work of deciphering and unearthing has been prodigious. The fact that I do not agree with certain general conclusions does not mean that I do not fully appreciate their contributions. Their expertise means that they are immersed in particular aspects of the work which they must fit into the accepted model or overall plan, without being in a position to reassess it. I would also like to thank John Bright for his clear exposition (with excellent datecharts) of that accepted model.

It is, nevertheless, particularly the people who have persisted in challenging the accepted view, the textbook version of Bronze Age history, to whom I am indebted and, most especially Immanuel Velikovsky, the pioneer, Professor Anati, Professor Cohen, Professor Cyrus Gordon, Philip Cohane and Julian Jaynes.

I am grateful to Heythrop College, the Warburg, and Dr. Williams Library.

On a more personal note, I would like to thank Peter James for being the first to publish a part of my work in the *SIS* review, Martin Sieff for his support and continuous flow of ideas, and his friend Marvin Luckerman, editor of *Catastrophism and Ancient History*. My thanks also go to Peter

James's friend who supplied the idea that Homer's description of the expedition to Egypt was related to the Pharaoh's victory over the sea peoples. I would also like to thank Marion Stancioff for her remarkable work on symbolism and David Croom for a second timely appearance; this time putting me in touch with Marion Russell. I am also deeply indebted to Fiona Brown for her careful work, checking, revising and polishing my manuscript.

Finally, I must thank Hélène on whom I have relied for so much help and understanding – not least her intelligent evaluation of my work.

The publisher and author are grateful to the Division of Christian Education of the National Council of the Churches of Christ for allowing up to 500 verses of their *Revised Standard Version of the Bible* (copyright 1946, 1952, 1971) to be used for scholarly interpretation or exposition; to Princeton University Press for permission to quote from *Ancient Near Eastern Texts: relating to the Old Testament*, 1950, ed. James B. Pritchard. Permission has been requested from Thames & Hudson to reproduce the illustration of pottery in *The Beaker Folk*, 1900, Richard Harrison; J. Richie, copyright holder of *Digging up Jericho*, 1900, Dame Kathleen Kenyon, to reproduce the illustration of pottery at Jericho.

INTRODUCTION

Between prehistory and history proper there lies an intermediate period whose literature strikes oddly on the modern ear, as if written in a slightly different key.

After thousands of years of silence, the voice of man reaches us for the first time across the millennia through the medium of writing. The long silent era of prehistory is over, but it is not yet the voice of modern man which reaches us.

For a period lasting more than 2,500 years, the literature throws light on an older mythological perspective rooted in cyclic time: the annual cycle of the year with its feasts and fasts, its processions and rituals, all arranged according to the phases of the moon, the solstices and equinoxes of the sun, and the cycle of the zodiac.

The starting point of this Age of Myth is the first picture-writing in Mesopotamia which remains undeciphered. According to legend, the Sumerians brought the art of writing with them when they joined the Semites to build that very early civilization on the banks of the Euphrates and the Tigris.

The Sumerians also influenced the Egyptians in prehistoric times, although a little later it was again the Semites – this time working hand-in-glove with the Hamites – who laid the foundations of the Pyramid Age there. A fair amount of their profound mythological literature has survived in one form or another.

This marked the beginning of a highly creative period for man in the Ancient Near East. Besides the art of writing, there were innovations in architecture, shipping, medicine, metalcraft, and almost every other aspect of life including warfare and law.

It was also the heyday of the Semites. They were centred in Western Asia, including Mesopotamia, Assyria, Syria and Old Phoenicia. The partially deciphered 'Linear A' writing suggests that they either formed an older stratum of the population in Greece and Crete, or else had a strong influence there. Prospecting for tin may have carried their seafarers far afield: amber from the Baltic, jade from China, and orientals at the Hittite court suggest contacts with Europe and the Far East. Cyrus Gordon is not alone in believing they reached the Americas 3,000 years before Columbus. The watershed at the end of this era, the Age of Myth, comes around 750 BC.

By then Homer's epics had reached their final form. Homer sang in the old tongue of a time when the imagination was still on an equal footing with the intellect, a time when men saw visions and spoke with the gods. This mentality is rare now. The old voice is still heard to this day in poetry, drama and ritual, but it is no longer on an equal footing with the prevailing voice. The dominant conscious attitude had changed.

It is a new voice that reaches us now, the voice of modern man, with his logical bias, his intellectual concepts and his sense of linear time – the historical perspective.

From about 750 BC there was a new widespread interest in history. In Mesopotamia, Egypt and Greece, chronicles were being compiled that were not so different from the much later Anglo-Saxon chronicle – or even modern records for that matter.

The Hebrews of the Levant were no exception to the general trend. Amos and Hosea wrote like modern men, concerned with social justice rather than myth and ritual, and Hebrew chroniclers compiled their great history. Like other nations they delved into archives of older material which they compiled and reshaped in response to the new demand for logic rather than mythology, for history rather than the annual cycle of ritual. They demythologized. By revising their material in the light of the more logical world view which was just emerging, the chroniclers found their mark; for many generations their work has had a profound influence on Western society through three major world religions.

But it is beginning to pall. It no longer meets our needs. That is partly because another change is now taking place: psychological man has been born, and the newly emerging psychological perspective values myth once more. The growing psychological need now is to recover content lost in the unconscious, and re-integrate it.

From this point of view the chroniclers may have done an injustice to the original material by attempting to suppress its mythological layers. But the process doesn't end there.

PART ONE

A Psychological View of the Bronze Age

= 1 =

THE LOST CHILDHOOD
OF MAN

The Cradle of the Unconscious

The Ancient Near East has been called the cradle of civilization. It could also be called the cradle of the unconscious.

I have been very much impressed and influenced by Julian Jaynes's extraordinary study of the origins of our modern conscious outlook: the birth of the conscious ego of modern man. He places that birth at around the beginning of the Classical Age of Greece. For him, Homer's era marks the watershed, when men still experienced life in the old mythological way. Up until that time, around 700 BC as Jaynes describes it, two centres of arbitration were struggling for supremacy: the imagination and the intellect. But from that time the intellectual ego got the upper hand and increasingly became the dominant conscious attitude. When the intellect won it was a great triumph for the human race, as it is today when a child reaches the age of reason and discernment. Stories often depict or reflect the psychological situation, and many stories tell the tale of the triumph of the heroic ego over the dragon of the unconscious. The gain for mankind has also been expressed in the grandeur of Classical Greece and Rome.

But the triumphant step forward was taken at considerable cost. The gain for the human psyche – the mind – also involved a loss. As with the child who loses its fairy-tale

3

world of wonder and imagination, so even at that time, 3,000 years ago, men seem to have been deeply aware of their loss. And their stories tell of it: Psyche – the soul – lost Eros, which foretells the conscious intellect prying too much into the affairs of the heart and casting its cold blight over the domains of feeling and appreciation. Orpheus lost Eurydice. And some scholars have suggested that the Hebrew account of The Fall, the story of how mankind lost paradise, originated in this period, where, in any case, it fits well.

What was lost had been expressed in the grandeur of civilization in the Bronze Age. The childhood of civilized man.

When civilized man came of age, his conscious ego emerged at the expense of its unconscious background. At first, much had to be deliberately rejected and repressed, but later it just got neglected. The older layers of our own minds were disowned.

Similarly a whole period of history was forgotten. The long period between the building of the pyramids and the fall of Tutankhamun's empire lay mostly buried. Until the last century, when Troy was excavated and hieroglyphs were deciphered, very little had been known about the Bronze Age. Only then did it begin to emerge from the mists of time as a truly magnificent era. Excavations began in earnest and continue still, rediscovering lost kingdoms and empires.

The activities of archaeologists digging up this earlier legendary age have coincided with the work of psychologists who are similarly unearthing the depths of the unconscious. And all the while, the prevailing conscious attitude has been showing signs of another change. There is growing dissatisfaction with the tyranny of the intellectual ego which has proved inadequate on its own. Its critical powers have been slowly corroding our powers of appreciation. Logical analysis dissects brilliantly but if this isn't balanced with an ability to synthesize, it can lead to a deadly disintegration of everything, including the psyche and society. The loss of feeling has dire consequences: without feeling you can't answer the question 'which?'. You don't know what to value. You can't relate. You can't even feel alive. Life itself has no value for you. Equally, without intuition, you can't answer the question 'why?'. You can't discern the meaning of life. So life becomes pointless. And man's creative potential turns negative and destructive.

Freud and Jung were pioneers, and many have followed, looking for the treasures buried in the depths of the psyche – its older part which was first diagnosed in hypnosis, but then investigated through dreams and imagination. And the ensuing work of depth psychology became the quest for the unconscious.

This quest has run parallel with the quest for remote antiquity. Beyond classical Greece and Rome, lies the Bronze Age with its different perspective which opens the way to still wider horizons.

But ordinary household history, the textbook version, still hardly penetrates beyond ancient Greece and Rome. Very few people would be able to name the main characters or the most important events of the Bronze Age.

What isn't appreciated enough is that, in cutting off this long period of remote antiquity and consigning it to oblivion, we are stunting our own story. It is ourselves we mutilate.

Those potentates who wanted history to begin with their reign and tried to erase from the record all previous events seem ridiculous. Yet we are inclined to do exactly the same, only a little more subtly. In the language of Jungian psychology, everything that is not accepted as part of the conscious ego, joins the unconscious shadow. In terms of history, the collective conscious attitude of a society accepts one part and leaves the rest in shadow.

With each generation the last regime, the last phase is blackened, darkened. The Renaissance left the previous era in shadow, the Dark Ages. And in the same way the Classical

Age of Greece and Rome has left the previous period in deep shadow.

This period was such a playful and inventive time that I cannot help thinking of it as the childhood of mankind. But it was no animal paradise that has been lost. It was a sophisticated and civilized world, but none the less the childhood of sophisticated and civilized man: when he learned to write for the first time and played with bricks and stones, albeit building them into domes, pillars and pyramids. He still had time for seven-day festivals with processions and night vigils. But above all, he still experienced life in terms of imagination, feeling and intuition: the mythical worldview, which has survived only in dreams in the night.

We experience tantalizing glimpses of this Age of Myth, which come in two forms. Either under a thin layer of soil that covers the mounds which are opened up by archaeologists to reveal the remnants of remote antiquity: bits and pieces that have survived. Or else as the living heritage of man, as preserved in his fairy tales, dramas, myths and religions: other shreds and tatters. Both sorts of evidence lie half buried in an underworld that reflects man's unconscious psyche, or soul.

Jung's depth psychology aims at relating conscious with unconscious. This is what brings wholeness and sanity. Part of this process lies in relating past to present, remote antiquity to the present time.

In recovering the lost childhood of man, we also rediscover a formative period for the human psyche. Learning about the way mankind developed before the conscious ego took command inevitably throws light on the way the human mind works now.

The sophisticated ego is a great prize. Whether it was acquired about 3,000 years ago or not, it has certainly been consolidating its domination of the psyche ever since that time. The danger is that it is becoming congealed. There is a growing need to relate back to a deeper unconscious level of life which is more direct, more feeling, with a natural grace and wisdom that is sometimes more appealing than the dazzling accomplishments of the intellectual.

In particular, the current prevailing Western mentality has lost the mythological worldview. It lies in the depth of the unconscious like a sleeping child. Whereas our intellectual and material functions are grey with exhaustion, the dormant functions of feeling and intuition are still as fresh as the child – at play in dreams.

However, it is not a question of swopping the analytical or critical mind for the mythological perspective, but of relating and integrating the two in a new psychological perspective, as if combining the present maturity of man with his own half-forgotten childhood.

The store of unconscious memories and images has been accumulating over many centuries. Just as evolution leaves its mark on the body which has gradually changed from sponge to thumb, from amoeba to eyeball, so evolution leaves its trace in the mind. Each century has left its mark in the living tissue. Each lifetime leaves its impact.

The ephemeral facts are digested and leave their enduring trace in the mind. Past history becomes present psychological reality. Life and history are lived out for the sake of the continuing human soul which is renewed and transformed, as expressed in the Cycle of Myth.

The Strata of the Mind
Jung compared the human psyche with ancient Rome, built layer upon layer. It is a good image.

The classical style dominates Rome, whether from antiquity or from its renaissance. But below the surface, somewhere in the foundations of Rome, are the mysterious Etruscans with their undeciphered script and their alleged connections with ancient Troy which was in the Pelasgian and Semite colony of Lydia. Straight away we enter the realms of myth: the mythical journey of Aeneas from the Ancient Near East via the Old Phoenician colony of Carthage, to Tuscany and Rome. Similarly, the analytical mind dominates the outlook of our Western society although historically our outlook has emerged from the symbolic mind, and psychologically it still is arising from there.

The mythological or symbolic mind works through visual images, dream-pictures, which express especially vividly feelings and intuitions. According to recent research, this imaginative side of the mind is located in the right hemisphere of the brain, which operates the less efficient left half of the body, whereas the logical and verbal side of the mind is normally located in the left hemisphere, operating the more efficient right half of the body.

From this it appears that the analytical mind is the more efficient and useful of the two, and fitter to survive. True. A more conscious logical outlook is more efficient and may even account for the success of the Romans in the Ancient world. But pursuing the analogy of the body and the mind which are so closely connected, just because the right arm is stronger, you would never consider letting your left arm wither away from neglect. Yet this is a very real danger with the mind. If the imagination were visible, nobody would want to let it shrivel and decay in front of their eyes, just because it wasn't quite as efficient or useful as the intellect.

It is not a question of one or the other; like the body, the mind is crippled unless all the parts work together.

Psychological Man
Prehistoric man inhabited the vast silent era of prehistory, in which the unconscious mind of man slowly took shape.

In the culminating twenty-five centuries of this long formative period of the unconscious, man has communicated something of this older mythological stratum of the mind. This is the legacy of Mythological man living in the Age of Myth.

Finally Modern man with his ego-consciousness emerged in the modern era, which has also lasted about twenty-five centuries. There is nothing wrong with his intellect or logic as such, but it is so exclusive; in particular it would like to exclude feeling and intuition.

Modern man is competitive and competes especially against Mythological man, for the most part with great success. The inner strife has overflowed socially in the extermination or indoctrination of peoples with the older mentality. Also in the conflicts of classical versus romantic, science versus religion, each of which is limited in its own way and excludes the interesting domains of the other. For the ego it is always a question of either/or, and the old ways must go.

So Mythological man has been pushed out on to the fringes of society or kept isolated from its main work. And this is only a superficial manifestation of what is going on at a deeper level, within the psyche, where the myth-making imagination is being repressed into the unconscious. There it behaves irrationally, erratically, even dangerously, giving the ego, especially the big social ego, good grounds for further repressive measures.

There is, however, a fourth man now emerging: Psychological man. Psychological man shows a newly awakening interest in his Mythological ancestor, who is still the lord of our unconscious minds, spinning the web of our fantasies and dreams.

If we try to piece together this Mythological man from his literature in the Bronze Age, it is not in order to go back and embrace his worldview once more. That would be undesirable, as well as impossible. It is not a question of either/or. It was never a question of either conscious or unconscious, any more than it is a question of preference of one period in history to the exclusion of another. It is rather a question of restoring the proper balance by gaining a balanced view of history which in turn affects the balance of the mind.

The conscious ego of Modern man is the wonderful late flowering of the older mind, but not the last word. The fruit is still to come.

From the psychological point of view, the three main

phases of man's historical development are still alive in us today. Prehistoric man embodies our vital, but basic, physical needs. Mythological man embodies our feelings and intuitions. And Modern man our intellect.

The reasonable hope is that psychology will be able to present our Mythological ancestor in a new light to the conscious ego, making the mythological layer of the mind more acceptable and so paving the way to synthesizing the three men in a fourth.

Meanwhile the bias remains. Nothing so far has prevented the logical mind from feeling threatened by the symbolic. This bias or prejudice against the symbolic is reinforced by what Jung has called 'the collective conscious attitude' of Western society. J. B. Priestley called it 'the fortress mentality'. Common sense has always been wary of the 'herd instinct' and maintained a sneaking respect for the dissident voice. There now, however, is a growing awareness of the dangers of what is called 'groupthink' in America. 'Groupthink' has been applied to the particular illusion of settling for safety in numbers and thinking that the majority must be right, thereby failing to assess the voice of the divergent thinker at its true worth. 'Groupthink' excludes the possibility of any new or truly original thought, which of its nature must start with the individual and gradually spread to the majority.

Until Freud's brilliant analysis of the psychological relevance of the Oedipus myth, the prevailing mood of the majority in Western society for more than 2,500 years had been logical and intellectual, with an abhorrence of myth.

For Modern man, with his conscious bias towards thinking, 'myth' has become synonymous with 'illusion' and 'fallacy'. To the logical mind it is antipathetic and seems to have no base. In terms of intellectual interests such as philosophy and history, it is nonsense. And this is perfectly valid from the intellectual point of view. It is one side of the story. One side of us inevitably feels this way. But this is a one-sided and, therefore, limited view.

If myth was the hub and focus of life for our ancestors, it is hardly surprising if it has some significance and value for their descendants. And from the psychological point of view, myth has once more become important.

Two Sources of the One Myth

My own investigations have centred on the relationship between Hebrew tradition as preserved in the Bible and the story of the rest of the Ancient Near East in the Bronze Age. It is this work especially that has led me to the conviction that there was once a single myth held by all civilized people, including the Hebrews. In fact, it is the Hebrew strand of the myth which has preserved it best, despite the fact that it has been drastically changed and often disguised as history, with divine figures frequently turned into mere mortals. In recovering the underlying myth in these texts, it is my sincere hope that we may retrieve the main thread which could join the modern era to the Age of Myth in remote antiquity. For me this work has provided a key which opens the door between two divergent worldviews: the logical and the mythological, the conscious and the unconscious.

These investigations involve showing the relationship between two distinct types of material from very different sources. One source is the archaeological evidence, such as fragments of literature from Egypt, Mesopotamia, Syria and Old Phoenicia, which throw direct light on the Bronze Age. These archaeological excavations and the work of deciphering the texts found only started in the last century. It is very recent, and it has taken place piecemeal, bit by bit. The bits have been found by chance – an arbitrary assortment. These are the dead myths, frozen in their original form, like parts of some mammoth. There has hardly been time to assemble a complete picture from these parts, let alone compare it with the picture that emerges from the other source of information.

The other source consists of documents that have continued to play a living part in cult and so, necessarily, have

evolved and changed with the changing beliefs and practices of that people. Recognizing the relationship between
the latter group and the former could be compared to trac-
ing the hereditary link between the living elephant and
the ancestral mammoth. One must take into account the
change of climate. In this case it is the universal tendency to
demythologize in the modern era. All the literature recovered
from the Bronze Age is profoundly mythological in tone, so
in order to relate the Hebrew stories to it these must be
re-mythologized; as only like can be related with like –
myth and legend with myth and legend. But once this is
done, the resemblance between the dead myths excavated,
and living myth preserved in cult, is striking.

My investigations have drawn me slowly, but irrevocably,
to the conclusion that these two sources are just two versions of the same story. One story which was the accepted
myth of the Ancient Near East in the Bronze Age and
from there carried far afield to outposts of the civilized
world.

Whereas in classical antiquity the Greeks could still rec-
ognize the underlying identity of their myth and that of
Egypt, in the case of the Hebrew version it was different.
There had been drastic religious reforms and the Hebrew
chroniclers, like true children of their time, had reclothed
their whole story in a new outer garment in order to present
it to a new audience, the new-born Modern man, with his
bias towards logic, linear time and history. This veneer,
this wrapping has kept the story isolated from the one great
universal myth of mankind. This myth is the very root of the
Sacred. Its many diverse tendrils bring life and nourishment
from the ground of the unconscious soul. Myth is, of its
nature, complex, like the tangled roots. Even one dream is
complicated, so how much more complex and compressed
is the universal myth of mankind? It is a complicated tangle
of roots but with many connections and interactions. And
all feeding the Tree of Life.

If the One God of later Judaism is compared to the trunk

of the Tree, then it has borne fruit on many branches of the different living religions, but the Tree depends on its ancient roots, just as the life of the individual ego depends on its unconscious background. These roots are twined and tangled in the old symbolic mind, with its mythological perspective.

The First of the Chroniclers

I want you to consider carefully the Hebrew chroniclers. This involves casting your mind back 2,500 years and more. You are getting near the cusp, the watershed at the beginning of the Modern era, with the Age of Myth lying in the past. I want to look at the Hebrew chroniclers from both points of view, both as the first of the historians and as the last of the mythmakers.

If we take the year 750 BC as the watershed, the coming of age of civilized man, with his adult interests in logic and history, this is when the chroniclers began their work, compiling and editing their material over a period of about 350 years (c. 750–400).

As I have already mentioned, their work was not unique, in the sense that they weren't the only ones. Within this same period, Herodotus, the so-called 'Father of History', was also at work, visiting Egypt to consult the priests and compiling his great history of the ancient world. In Assyria there was a similar movement gathering archives and delving into the past. A little later Manetho would write his great chronicle of Egypt.

Every nation was beginning to recover from the disastrous break, the Early Dark Ages, in which the Bronze Age civilization had been shattered. The period of the break is obscure of its nature: a 'dark' age. With the decline of culture, no records were kept. It seems that the art of writing was forgotten for a while. So it is by no means easy to reconstruct this period even now, with all the archaeological evidence. It is by no means sure how long it lasted. What is absolutely true is that the Bronze Age

13

civilization was smashed, whether by natural catastrophe, human agency or both.

The glorious era of the Bronze Age had lasted 2,500 years and more from the rise of the Sumerians to the fall of Tutankhamun's empire, and included the wonders of the Pyramid Age, Mycenean Greece, Minoan Crete and the Hittite empire. But all that was nearly forgotten, swept into oblivion during the Dark Ages which followed. Only the remnant of it survived, shreds and tatters which the new breed of historians tried to cobble together in their own fashion, and which the old dramatists like Sophocles used in their very different fashion.

Bearing this in mind, let us look again more closely at the Hebrew chroniclers, and most especially at the scribes and librarians in charge· of the archives in the reign of King Josiah (640–609 BC). This is a well-documented reign. All kinds of small incidents were being documented and recorded. And this had already been going on for about a hundred years. Records had been kept because there had, once again, been kings and courtiers and, therefore, scribes to keep such records. The first of such scribes might in their turn have been able to reconstruct another century or so back before their time from the stories of the old men and from the buildings which would tell a tale. King Omri's new capital city at Samaria and a number of rebuilding projects marked the beginning of the recovery after the Dark Ages.

Part of this recovery and rebuilding programme included repairs to the ancient Temple in Jerusalem, in the reign of King Josiah. From the descriptions we have, we know this temple was built with megalithic stones in the style of Bronze Age buildings. The stones of the 'Wailing Wall' standing in Jerusalem to this day are of this same type. Behind one of those stones during the course of repairs to the temple, a book was found. It is described as the book of the law, the Torah, and the book of the covenant. This book had preserved the ancient rituals, including how to celebrate the Passover, 'for no such Passover had been kept since the days of the Judges'. It is possible that the vast stones of the Temple provided just the niche which favoured the freak preservation of an important document surviving from an earlier era, describing the ancient rituals and myths of the Hebrew people. A scroll, or a number of scrolls on paper, parchment or leather, preserved despite the damp climate of Western Asia which did not favour the preservation of such documents in the ordinary way.

The chroniclers themselves devote two chapters of their work to describing this incident in great detail. Part of the detail is concerned with Josiah's reforms, which also feature in the contemporary prophecies of Jeremiah. The Queen of Heaven, once honoured with crescent cakes and the cult of the zodiac, was condemned. The chariots of the sun-god were burned. The prophets who interpreted dreams were no longer tolerated. It would seem that the gods and goddesses revered by the whole Semite world in the Bronze Age were now being subjected to sweeping reforms. We shall return to this vital issue and give it proper consideration in due course.

Meanwhile, whether the chroniclers were working from an ancient text preserved in very special circumstances or not, they were certainly working from older documents. They say so themselves and mention such books as *The War Songs of the Lord* and *The Book of Iddo the Seer*. They were inevitably delving into archives, compiling, collating and revising the material, with the intention of presenting the complete picture, the whole history of their people, from the very beginning.

The Third Gap
But did the chroniclers take into account the Dark Ages?

Just as it is still difficult, in spite of all our archaeological expertise, to establish exactly what happened in those Dark Ages and precisely how long they lasted, would it have been any easier for the chroniclers themselves to reconstruct what happened? Could they have overlooked a few hundred years? Does their text conceal an unacknowledged gap – a time gap?

Of course I am already convinced of this, but for the moment I only want you to toy with the idea of such a gap. If you had a selection of very ancient and more recent stories with a gap between the two, nothing would disappear as easily as that gap.

There are two other significant gaps in the chroniclers' story. The first is near the beginning and the other is near the end. The first gap is accounted for in a single sentence: the Hebrew ancestors spent four hundred years in Egypt, between the time of Joseph and the time of Moses. And that's all we know. Imagine what would happen if that sentence had been left out and the story skipped from Joseph to a pharaoh who didn't know Joseph. We might easily assume that Joseph had lived a generation or so before Moses. Another such gap is after the fall of Jerusalem in 587 BC and coincides with a period of foreign domination and exile. What I am proposing is a third gap, unacknowledged by the chroniclers like the gap at the end of their tale, but coming right in the middle. We could call it the middle gap. To be precise, it comes between the end of Jehosaphat's reign and the beginning of Omri's reign and, like the last gap, coincides with a period of foreign domination and exile followed by the Dark Ages. Just suppose that for a while there were no kings. Then there would be no court and no scribes: no regnal years, and no scribes to record them anyway. But keeping count of the reigns of the kings was the usual way of reckoning the passing years.

What I am suggesting is that from the time when the West Semites were defeated by Tuthmosis III at the Battle of Megidde and all their princes were carted into exile, while puppet kings were installed in Jerusalem, as mere regents of ruling foreign powers, the records were no longer kept. Stories about the ensuing Dark Ages were scanty and unreliable. We can glean a little information from other books, from prophecies and oracles and psalms of lament, as well as from the archaeological record and other outside sources, but 'when all is done dismaying lacunae and baffling problems remain.'[1] We shall reconsider the evidence for this gap in *Interim Section 3*.

But, toying with the idea a little longer, it seems to me that even if the chroniclers were aware of such a gap in their knowledge, there is one very good reason why they wouldn't want to acknowledge it. Part of their whole endeavour was to show the direct line of succession from David and Solomon to their own monarchs. To be vague about this would throw doubt on the legitimacy of their king. So consider the possibility that they delved as far as they could into the recent past, as far back as Omri, and simply hooked these stories onto earlier stories from remote antiquity, stories from the Bronze Age which had been preserved one way or another.

The line of succession of their kings had to be assured at all costs. The cost in this case may have been a considerable distortion of history which has left most of the Hebrew story floating in the vacuum of the Dark Ages, instead of being firmly anchored in the Bronze Age. And this, in turn, has resulted in cutting off our religions from their roots in the Age of Myth.

The Last of the Mythmakers

Julian Jaynes suggests that the abhorrence of myth and of the mythological perspective would have been at its most intense when the conscious ego was first struggling for supremacy and still extremely vulnerable. And that is precisely the time when the Hebrew chroniclers were writing. Their loathing of the old mythological worldview is confirmed by the picture of reforming zeal in the reigns of Hezekiah and Josiah at the time of the prophet Jeremiah.

Nevertheless, anyone who examines the Hebrew chronicle carefully can quite easily discern an older mythological substratum showing through the veneer of history. It is not new to notice this. The Jesuit, Iganz Goldziher, published his

Mythology among the Hebrews in 1877, in which he detects the underlying mythological material right up to the time of the Judges. More recently, works like *Israelite Religion* by Helmer Ringgren show, for example, that personal names right up into the reigns of David and Solomon still honoured the old Semite pantheon of gods and goddesses, as was customary among the Semites in the Bronze Age. And if you work back through the Bible from the time of the chroniclers, you quickly come upon this older mythological substratum in the story of Elijah, or Elias, who goes up to heaven in a fiery chariot and so resembles Helios, the sun-god of Greece. Just as Homer's epics mark the end of the Age of Myth in Greece, so the story of Elijah may be used to mark the same watershed in the Levant.

It may be relevant to note here that the stories of Elijah and Elisha are the last of the traditional stories that feature in the Koran as well as in the Hebrew Bible. Could this mean they derive from traditions held in common by the whole Semite world at one time? Perhaps in the Bronze Age, before the coalition of Semite powers was shattered. Could there be a relationship between the 'Habiru', or Hebrews, who disappeared at the end of the Bronze Age 'when men became rare as fine gold' and the 'Arabu', or Arabs, who appear after the Dark Ages? And does this throw any light on the so-called 'Lost Tribes'? Here it is simply a question of distinguishing between an older stratum of the Bible and its later layers and embellishments, between an ancient testament salvaged from remote antiquity and a merely Old Testament, the product of classical antiquity.

The difference between the two seems to show in the difference between legendary figures like Elijah and more historical figures like Amos and Hosea, or Jeremiah. And again in the difference between kings cast in the modern mould, like Josiah, and the ancient legendary kings like David and Solomon. David, with his bow and his mighty men who slew tens of thousands, whose saga could have been sung at any ancient banquet. Or Solomon, with his hundreds of wives and concubines, who had thousands of cattle slaughtered for the gargantuan feast to dedicate his Temple, a tale which is reminiscent of a Bronze Age text found at Ugarit about the dedication of the Temple to Baal Saphon.

But such differences might appear much more striking if we had the original documents. All the time we are confronted by a document that has been revised and revised again, by men working in the modern era, modern men with their own particular mental bias, a predilection for history rather than myth, an inclination to gloss over the differences and rework legend into a semblance of fact.

Only by taking this bias into account would it be possible to reconstruct the underlying mythological material from which they were working, which they were reworking into their Chronicle of the Hebrews.

Whereas history is concerned with linear time, myth is firmly set in the annual cycle of the year and celebrates cyclic time. It is the words and rubrics of that recurring cycle. So much so that some people have made the mistake of thinking myth is *about* the cycle of the year: an over-complicated and rather obscure way of telling you when to sow and when to reap, and what to put aside for next year's planting. The annual cycle is merely the appropriate setting for the perennial concern of man, centred on his relationship with the universe and the powers that govern it. The true context of all the older stories in the Bible is this recurring cycle of mythological time. No one would want to dispute this. The same annual cycle of feasts and fasts and commemorations has been celebrated without interruption to this day. It is the fullest account of any ancient cycle to be preserved or reconstructed.

The point which has not been sufficiently appreciated is that under the historical veneer, what is really being described is not the events, but their annual re-enactment, their ritual celebration, rather than the historical events themselves. It is the story of processions that took place

19

every year, of what happened on the days of observance and, in particular, it is a witness of the words prescribed for the rituals. In other words it is the enduring myth of the Hebrew-speaking people.

For example, seven days have been allocated to celebrate the Creation. Another forty days' observance, probably synchronized with the rainy season, may have commemorated the Pluvial Age for all we know. Gathering the harvest into the granaries each year may have gradually reshaped the story of Joseph. The story of the Plagues in Egypt has taken the form of a dramatic ritual, with priests intoning and people responding. Processions following clouds of incense by day and torches of flames by night may have marked the ritual inauguration of days of solemn observance that recalled the trek out of Egypt and the gruelling years in the desert where a whole generation died. And the dismal wail of the shofar trumpets simulated the groaning of the earth before an earthquake – the earthquake which felled the city walls of Jericho and opened the way to the conquest of the land in which they lived and where they performed these annual rituals and official celebrations. What I am suggesting is that this cycle of mythical time has been superficially flattened out and made to look like linear or historical time by scribes of the modern era anxious to satisfy the new thirst for history, rather than myth.

For our point of view, now, such a tampering with the ancient sacred texts would be unthinkable and, indeed, that is the attitude that has prevailed for over 2,000 years, during which time no one has thought to revise the Bible or add to it. The question is, did the chroniclers share this point of view? The evidence suggests they did not. Their analytical and historical perspectives were newly acquired and cannot be assessed by our criteria or compared with our own academic standards. They were still mythmakers at heart, albeit the last of the mythmakers. The mythmaker, by contrast, continually adapts his material to current and local psychological needs, to the immediate here and now. Their contemporaries demanded history and so the old material was recast as history. This means it has had two layers ever since: the superficial historical layer which appeals to the conscious ego precisely because it has been stripped of embarrassing mythological encumbrances; but also another layer which appeals directly to the unconscious which was shaped in the old mythological era and still functions in the symbolic mode.

In this way the structure of the book exactly matches the double structure of the psyche, so it is no wonder the chroniclers' work has held many generations enthralled and may continue to appeal to 'children not yet born'.

A New Look at the Bronze Age

My main interest is in the story of religion and the relationship between the ancient roots of the sacred, and the living tree. At first glance, Hebrew religion would seem to be isolated from these universal roots, insulated against them. Though the Hebrews were situated at the hub and crossroads of the ancient world, they would appear to have developed a religion peculiar to themselves, unrelated to the beliefs of their neighbours.

Although their story claims to go back to the very beginning, according to our textbook version of history they were late arrivals on the scene: the Sumerians had been and gone; the Egyptians were at the tail end of their greatest period with the New Empire of the Pharaohs like Akhenaten and Tutankhamun; the first pyramid was already 1,500 years old at the time when Moses is generally supposed to have left Egypt. The Dark Ages were about to descend on the whole of the Ancient Near East just as they entered the Levant, and most of their story takes place in this vacuum, or so we are led to suppose. The same vacuum that nurtured and insulated their religion. The vacuum of the Dark Ages, when the art of writing appears to have been forgotten so that there are

21

no outside records to refute the Hebrew story. But there are also no records to corroborate it.

The result is that we have a Hebrew story set against a vacuum. This in itself presents the first problem: why was it only the Hebrews who were so busy recording their history throughout the Dark Ages, while their neighbours kept no records, and seem to have forgotten how to write? Then there are other problems. From the beginning of the Bronze Age, the same population inhabited the Levant. These inhabitants were Semites, with a consistent culture throughout that long period. This means there is no corroborating evidence for a major conquest. Historians like Martin Noth have speculated that there must have been an infiltration of forces who huddled round the old towns and gradually got absorbed into the older population, leaving no trace in the archaeological record. Perhaps. The legendary reigns of David and Solomon are also set in the context of the Dark Ages. Their trading ships were away for three years and all the kings of the earth paid tribute, but Dame Kathleen Kenyon can find no trace of any imported objects for that period.

At the moment what we have is the Hebrew story floating in a vacuum and a Bronze Age people without a story. Let's take a closer look at the people. The West Semites, living in the Levant from before 2000 BC. What language did they speak? What were their customs? What was their religion? What can we glean about them from the archaeological record? The chroniclers could have turned myth into history and feasts and fasts into facts. They could have hammered the cycle of time into a straight line, linear time. With this in mind, we shall continue to toy with the idea that, by imposing a rigid chronology on their tale, they may have inadvertently sewn up a gap, a gap without which the nucleus of historical material which was the cause for annual celebrations floats in a vacuum, unsubstantiated by the archaeological evidence.

This gap has disappeared completely between the lines of

the text. It might have remained undetectable, but for other factors which point inexorably towards its existence.

From the West Semites Comes Silence

The pyramids are said to have been built at the centre of the landmass of the whole globe. Whether that is so or not, Western Asia is like the crossroads at the Ancient World: it is the hub of three continents: Asia, Africa and Europe.

In particular, the Levant and Syria guard the routes between Europe, Mesopotamia and Egypt. In other words, they controlled all roads north, south and east and their great ports on the Mediterranean gave them further control of all routes west, especially in the Middle Bronze Age.

From the east, from Mesopotamia, voices reach us across the chasm of time, voices incised into clay thousands of years ago and rising from the clay to reach us. We may not know the exact pronunciation of the words, but in every other way it is like finding a very ancient gramophone record, as the meaning comes through clearly enough. From the south, from Egypt, dried fragments of paper serve the same purpose and the voices reach us again. From the north, from Syria, word has reached us only recently with the discovery of two great libraries, at Ugarit and Ebla. From the west, from Crete, we also have word, but we can't understand it yet. It is in the undeciphered script, 'Linear A'.

But from the very centre of this picture, from the inhabitants of the interior of the Levant in the Middle Bronze Age, comes silence. We can glean a little about them from the archaeological record and piece it together with what we know about them from their neighbours, but of their side of the story we know nothing.

It would be good to know what they have to say of themselves, they are an interesting people at a key place and a key time in history. But unfortunately it is becoming increasingly unlikely that we shall ever hear their voice, their story. The archaeological excavation of the area has been extensive, intensive, and has failed to divulge a single text. Just a few characters from a very ancient form of the Hebrew alphabet, the so-called Sinaitic script, found in Sinai and Gezer. Tantalizing. It means these West Semites were literate, but their literature is presumed to have been written on paper, parchment or leather, which has not survived in the comparatively damp climate of Western Asia.

The silence will reverberate forever. Unless, that is, we already have their voice (possibly found in the nick of time, preserved against odds in a niche behind one of the great stones of the Temple complex in Jerusalem), albeit revised and somewhat garbled by later generations of scribes, but there none the less, perhaps already on your shelves as well as on the bedside locker of many dreary hotel rooms, supplied free by the Bible Society.

The place is right. The stories have much in common. The story of the West Semites pieced together from the archaeological fragments has much in common with the story told by the Hebrew chroniclers. Only the time is wrong. The dates cannot be synchronized. The chronology is haywire.

If you pick up any textbook version of the history of the Ancient Near East, you will find out quite quickly that these West Semites, though they had much in common with the Hebrews of biblical tradition, lived a thousand years too early. For example, it is possible that these West Semites arrived in the Levant during the period of hiatus, between the Early Bronze Age and the Middle Bronze Age. In this period there was a series of terrible earthquakes in the Jordan rift, deep below sea level, where Jericho stood. These successive earthquakes brought down the walls several times and each time the inhabitants rebuilt them, even stronger than before. The last set of walls fell, but were never rebuilt because nomads swept in, slaughtered the inhabitants, camped on the site and buried their dead in nearby hillside tombs. But if you open the *Penguin Dictionary of Archaeology* at the entry *Jericho* you will discover that 'these fallen walls found by Garstang are now known to be a millennium too early to be associated with Joshua's attack.'[2] Maybe. Or maybe Joshua's attack took place a thousand years earlier than was previously supposed.

Even by themselves these walls demand to be taken seriously as possible corroboration of a story which makes so much of them falling. Even if this piece of evidence stood alone, it would be by no means far-fetched to suggest this incident could have prompted annual celebrations with processions and the blowing of ram's horns to simulate the sound of the earthquake which brought down the walls, and so became part of the cult of the people. And it is this ceremony which is described in the Book of Joshua.

But this incident does not stand alone. In this same period of hiatus there are three other pieces of evidence that tend to corroborate the Hebrew stories in the context of these much earlier dates. There are two accounts of a catastrophe in Egypt which have much in common with the account of the Plagues, as Immanuel Velikovsky first pointed out. There is also a freak occupation of the Negeb, which Rudolph Cohen, in the *Biblical Archaeology Review*, relates tentatively to the story of the Exodus. And finally, there is Emmanuel Anati's archaeological investigation of Har Karkom which, in his book, *The Mountain of God*, he identifies with Mount Sinai, which was an important place of worship at the end of the Early Bronze Age but not later. He suggests, therefore, that the Exodus took place a thousand years earlier than is currently supposed.

These recent investigations have yet to be assimilated into the textbook version of history. And the repercussions will take decades or even centuries to work out.

But meanwhile these events seem to provide an anchor for the Hebrew story and it is this anchor, in turn, which necessitates a gap later in the Hebrew account. It is the chronology of the Hebrew chroniclers which cannot be trusted. The historical nucleus of their story was preserved in the annual rites and cult of their people, but their chronology was imposed later without due regard for a gap in their knowledge, which coincided with a dismal era for their people. There was nothing worth recording and no one to record it, as the tragic defeat of the Hebrews followed by the Dark Ages affected them no less than the rest of the Ancient Near East.

So long as there was no alternative chronology, each new archaeological find, each new fragment of information, had to be accommodated, and whenever the new data didn't fit the old model, there had to be an explanation, however far-fetched. Only by proposing a new overall model to work from can we see that the very bits and pieces which have been fitted so awkwardly into the old model are the very pieces that fall most satisfactorily into place in the new model, or overall plan. It is important to glimpse the plan as a whole first, which involves a rather generalized picture: the skeletal framework of the story into which the individual bricks can be placed, or the bare bones on which the flesh can be hung.

The next few pages will serve to sketch in this outline of the story of the West Semites, who were the earliest branch of Semites to speak Hebrew. If the skeletal structure of their story corresponds to the main features of the story preserved in later Hebrew tradition, if we can identify these West Semites with the Hebrews, then we shall know a great deal more about the roots of Hebrew religion as it flourished in Egypt in the Old Kingdom, and in the Levant in the Middle Bronze Age. An abundance of outside evidence will lend considerable weight to earlier attempts to detect a mytholical substratum to the religion of the Bible, the myth held in common by the Semite world, and disseminated far afield, in the Age of Myth.

Semite-Hamite Origins

In order to make bronze you need tin, which is a rare commodity, and if it was found at all in the Ancient Near East, it was not there in sufficient quantities to meet the demand. So prospecting for tin may have been the initial incentive which lured mankind to a great voyage of discovery. What did exist was the technology to sail; it has been demonstrated that the ocean-going vessels, manned by twenty men, as depicted in the pyramids, could have sailed to the ends of the earth.

At the very beginning of the Early Bronze Age, there was already an old city at Jericho, the oldest city in the world so far excavated, where the inhabitants had grown prosperous trading in the treasures of the Dead Sea: sulphur for making fire; salt for flavouring boiled food; and bitumen for caulking boats.

In so far as civilization is the story of city life, this walled city with terraced gardens, a tower and spiral staircase, marks the beginning of civilization. As far as we can tell from their religious practices and various other indications, the inhabitants were Semite or Hamite. Semite and Hamite are related languages that stem from a common parent language, but the two language groups had separated and evolved distinct characteristics in prehistoric times.

From the beginning of the Bronze Age it seems to have been the Semite branch which produced the great seafarers, whether based in the Levant, the direct ancestors of the Phoenicians who supplied Egypt with cedarwood from Lebanon, or based in the Delta region of Egypt which supported a large Semite population living side by side with the Hamite population. The Sumerians had also been an influence there in prehistoric times.

The Age of Myth opens with the first writing in the world, in Sumerian, and just before that came the first picture-writing, not yet deciphered, and the early cylinder seals and stamp seals. According to Sumerian legend they arrived with the art of writing, but in the absence of any earlier writing anywhere in the world, this seems unlikely for the time being. Again, according to the Sumerians themselves, the earliest kings were Semites: that is, they had Semite names like Gilgamesh, and it is more than likely that the Semite population was already long established when the

Sumerians arrived (*c.* 3500 BC). Their origin is still a mystery but their agglutinative language is related to Tamil-Indian and the evidence of the cylinder seals suggests that this early civilization practised yoga: one seal depicts a figure sitting cross-legged with what E. A. S. Butterworth has identified as the six chakras (the six centres of consciousness in yoga) arranged around him. Semites and Sumerians appear to have mingled peacefully and produced many cultural and technological innovations.

These same innovations reached Egypt as a result of Sumerian and Semite influences, and bore fruit there in the splendour of the Pyramid Age (*c.* 2700-2300 BC). At the very beginning of the Pyramid Age, an individual emerges in the human story, the legendary Imhotep, first of not more than twenty commoners in the whole long history of Egypt ever to be ranked with kings and pharaohs, first as semi-divine, and later full deity. He was the master-builder of the first step pyramid, a magician and astronomer, renowned for his wisdom. As the vizier of King Djoser, he brought to an end a seven-year famine. He was the father of Egyptian medicine which consisted (like our psychotherapy) of healing dreams and dream interpretation. Many temples were dedicated to him, where such healing dreams took place, including one at Anu ('On' in Hebrew tradition).

By the end of the Pyramid Age, there was a large population of Semites in the delta, many of them living in cities that numbered 60,000 inhabitants and more.

The first mention of the 'Hapiru', or Hebrews, is from an Egyptian document of this period.

Who Were the Hebrew-Speaking People?

The usual way of identifying a people, once the prehistoric period is over, is by language group. Yet, by some oversight, there seems to have been no attempt to identify the Hebrews with the Hebrew-speaking people in this ordinary way.

We have already mentioned the general spread of the major language groups in the Bronze Age: Tamil-Sumerian;

Semite-Hamite; and Indo-European. Within the Semite group in the Ancient Near East, there are three main subdivisions. First, the Akkadian-speaking Semites from Mesopotamia, whose language was also used as a diplomatic language for the whole Ancient Near East in much of the Bronze Age, so there is a considerable body of texts in this language. Secondly, there are the Northwest-Semite dialects, with the principal texts coming from the library recently excavated at Ebla in Syria, and the other library discovered fifty years ago at Ugarit on the coast in Old Phoenicia. The third language group is the West Semite, or Hebrew-speaking group. The only text in this language is the Hebrew Bible. But the Hebrew-speaking people, identified by their names only, were settled in the Levant from 2100 BC, and may have been identical with the 'Torc' people who invaded two centuries earlier.

The difference between Akkadian, Northwest Semite, and West Semite, or Hebrew, is roughly equivalent to the difference between the Romance languages, Latin, Italian and Spanish.

So how do these differences arise in general? And how and when, in particular, did Hebrew become a separate language with distinct characteristics? There are two main factors. A language may evolve distinct characteristics after a sufficiently long period of isolation from the parent language, but what speeds up the process is the influence of some other language group, from which new words and usages are accepted.

Living in close contact with the Sumerians and using their method of writing undoubtedly influenced Akkadian-Semite. It may have been a similar exposure to the Indo-European Hurrians which affected Northwest Semite and lent to it particular characteristics. And in the case of Hebrew, it would appear to be the influence of Hamite, or Egyptian, over a number of centuries which contributed to its particular distinctive qualities.

Where do we find the first traces of this specifically

Hebrew language? G. A. Barton couldn't be sure whether the Semites in the Delta during the Pyramid Age were Akkadian- or Hebrew-speaking. Could this be the period of 400 years when Akkadian developed into Hebrew? There is one piece of evidence that strongly supports this otherwise delicate thread, and that is the Hebrew alphabet. The debt of the Hebrew alphabet to Egyptian hieroglyphs (especially when these are used for the phonetic transcription of foreign names) is generally acknowledged. And the oldest examples of characters from this alphabet are from Sinai and Gezer in the Middle Bronze Age (*c.* 1800 BC).

It is natural to assume that these fragments of the oldest alphabet were the work of the West Semites who spoke and wrote a language closely akin to Hebrew. Any differences between their language and biblical Hebrew would be more than accounted for by the thousand-year period which divides their era from the time when the final version of the Hebrew Bible was composed.

So who were these West Semites? What did this Hebrew-speaking people do? When we have reconstructed their story, we shall be in a position to decide whether there is any connection between their history and the nucleus of historical fact (preserved from generation to generation in the annual cult and ritual and combined with other stories and written texts) in the Hebrew Bible.

From Egypt to Empire-Builders

There is evidence to suggest that the terrible catastrophes at the end of the Age of Taurus (*c.* 2300 BC) may have affected the whole world. Certainly they brought to an end the long period of stability in Egypt. From there come vivid accounts of 'grief stalking the land' where famine and pollution devastated its people.

It is still not finally settled whether Sargon the Great, who founded the Semite kingdoms of Agade and Asshur, had any connection with the downfall of Egypt at the end of the Pyramid Age or not. He was alleged to have made history and also kept historical records; the great law-codes of Mesopotamia date from soon after his time. There is an ancient legend about him as a baby being floated on the waters in a basket of reeds sealed with bitumen. There is also an extensive text which has survived about a longer period he spent in the desert.

At this time there was a freak occupation of the Negeb desert where a vast horde of people lived for less than a century using advanced irrigation techniques to conserve what little water there was, and worshipping at the ancient site of Har Karkom, where they built a twelve-pillared temple.

Were these the same people who took advantage of an earthquake to invade Jericho, who destroyed Ai and subsequently attacked and burnt every Early Bronze Age site so far investigated?

Their tombs, between Jericho and Mamre, have provided examples of seven distinct types of burial custom, for instance, the dagger and bead types. The burials in general have much in common with contemporary Egyptian burials – except that there are no images of any gods in the tombs.

From the archaeological evidence alone we cannot be certain what, if any, is the connection between these Torque people who lived nomadically for about two centuries and the people who settled and rebuilt the towns from c. 2100 BC. K. Kenyon thinks the rebuilding programme originated in Gubna and spread from there.

Soon after this, traces of the earliest alphabet, as well as the names of places and people, began to emerge which indicates the presence of the Hebrew-speaking people, variously called the Asiatics, the West Semites ('Amurru') or Hebrews ('Habiru' or occasionally 'Hapiru') by their neighbours. Although they form a recognizably distinct language group they are not unrelated to the other Semite powers, including Agade and Asshur.

Towards the end of the Middle Bronze Age a loose coalition of Semite powers was consolidated into a formidable empire, the first of its kind on earth. It was founded with the aid of the new Asiatic or composite bow made of sinew, horn and wood and the newly-domesticated horse, harnessed to war chariots. According to Manetho, the Egyptian chronicler, Salitis was the first king of this 'Hyksos', or 'foreign', empire, which appears to have stretched from the Nile to the Euphrates with a road and fortress towns built all along the route between the two, with their distinctive plastered slopes to protect the ramparts from battering rams or siege towers. There were important cities at Gezer, Megiddo and especially Hazor where the fortifications were on a grander scale than ever before or since in the area. The name of their most renowned king has been found far afield at Knossus, in Crete, and in Baghdad, east of the Tigris, leading to wild speculations about a far-flung empire on which the last word yet remains to be said. Another of their kings built, in Avaris, 'a temple of fair and everlasting beauty next to the house of the king'.

From Empire to Armageddon

Whatever the scale of this empire, it didn't last long, in fact, no more than two centuries. The kings traded in the horse and chariot. In this way they acquired great wealth, but at the same time the original source of their power passed into the hands of their enemies who returned to plunder their gains. In Mesopotamia, Hammurabi's Babylon fell to the Mitanni. And almost simultaneously the 'foreign rulers' were driven out of Egypt. According to the Egyptian chronicler, Manetho, when they left Egypt they went on to found Jerusalem, and the early terraced fortifications of Jerusalem date from this period.

A century or so later, Thutmose III pursued them into their own country and inflicted a crushing defeat at the Battle of Megiddo (c. 1468 BC). He took many slaves with names that W. F. Albright has identified with names that also occur in the Bible: Samson, Hodaviah, etc. And the booty which he took back from the Levant, as depicted in the stones of Karnak Temple, suggests the 'legendary' wealth of the King and princes that he plundered. This wealth was used in building the new empire of the Pharaohs, and remnants of it may have survived in the tomb of Tutankhamun.

This battle marked the end of the heyday of the Semites in general and the West Semites in particular. Their domains were carved up between the Egyptians and the Indo-European Hittites and Mitanni, all of whom took many Habiru (Hebrew) slaves. The Hebrew-speaking people had been crushed. The foreign powers installed puppet kings to rule over them in their own country. These puppet kings wrote to Akhenaten for help in crushing the last remaining pockets of Hebrew resistance, led by Abdi-ashirta and Aziru.

Meanwhile, in the far north,the more extensive use of iron heralded the beginning of the Iron Age, when the Celtic-Vedic people (riding mounted on horseback for the first time in history) conquered the world, from Ireland to India. They pushed down into Italy and Greece. The older population of Greece appears to have been driven out. Moving by sea and land, they destroyed the cities of Western Asia from Troy to Tyre. These 'sea peoples' were halted at the gates of Egypt and driven back into Philistia, where they settled. Shortly after this the Dark Ages descended on the Ancient Near East, the period of obscurity.

This brings to an end the Bronze Age, one of the most glorious eras in human history.

A Note on Armageddon

Armageddon still plays a part in the popular imagination, although it is only mentioned once in the Apocalypse (16/16) as the Great Victory at the End of Time, when some past defeat will be gloriously reversed.

Theologians have suggested this refers to the defeat of King Josiah at a battle at Megiddo which had no effect on the course of history. I doubt it. At most, this new defeat may have refreshed the collective memory of the crushing defeat of the Hebrew-speaking people at the hands of Tuthmosis III, from which they never recovered. This was truly the end of the world for the Hebrew people. Their name Hapiru, or Habiru, is recorded for the last time in the Late Bronze Age.

This was *the* Battle of Megiddo (*c*. 1468 BC) which is never to be forgotten, inscribed indelibly on the collective imagination, and still waits for Armageddon, part of the oral myth of a people.

The Semite world of the Habiru was shattered, and remained fragmented for two thousand years, until the rise of Islam reunited the Semite world of the Arabu.

Conclusion

The central aim of this book is to restore a portion of the Hebrew papers to their proper context in remote antiquity and thereby recover the ancient roots of Hebrew religion buried in an Age of Myth, thus restoring those roots to the living tree. By acknowledging and becoming conscious of the broader universal base of myth underlying the established religions, it is my sincere hope that those people who are more captivated by the Sumerian, Egyptian and Greek contributions to the story of civilization and religion will see the real significance of the Hebrew contribution in this context. I would also hope that those already devoted to the Hebrew kings and sages will re-evaluate the wider significance of their contribution in relation to an earlier phase of human development, which corresponds to an older substratum of the human soul.

In this first chapter I have worked backwards from the present psychological worldview. I have suggested that our logical and historical bias has been the prevailing conscious attitude for more than 2,500 years. But it is not a balanced view. It condemns imagination, feeling and intuition as expressed in the mythological perspective of an earlier age which was the formative period of our own unconscious. Uncovering and bringing to light the different layers of the unconscious has coincided with digging down into the carefully stratified layers of civilization in the Near East, and with bringing to light their archives and myths. I have also looked at the nature of some of this mythological material. In the second section I have suggested a new model for Bronze Age history. I have tried to present the overall picture, the skeletal framework, the bare bones. In subsequent chapters I shall be looking at particular details in the context of this model. I intend to start with the known facts, then look at the myths and legends which may have arisen from these facts, and present my own speculations and conclusions. I shall return to the psychological significance of the Age of Myth at the end.

This book is no more than a pilot scheme, a preliminary survey reconnoitring a vast area. I intend only to present the fruit of my work, my findings, rather than try to substantiate them. If some of the material is speculative, that is because the necessary preliminary work of conjecture has too often been skimped: Karl Popper shows the vital importance of this hypothetical work in his *Conjecture and Refutation*. So far, disproportionate effort has been lavished on substantiating premature conclusions in an effort to buttress the old model of the Bronze Age whenever it looks shaky. And, in particular, academic standards of historical accuracy have been projected back onto the Hebrew chroniclers, crediting them with chronological and geographical accuracy on the one hand, and discrediting the cornerstones of their story on the other. These cornerstones which take up a large proportion of their story are: Joseph; The Plagues; The Conquest; and the empire of David. We might justifiably expect to find archaeological or literary corroboration of these events as, indeed, we do in the Bronze Age, but not later.

What follows is a description of my efforts to reassemble a

gigantic puzzle. As you may remember, assembling a jigsaw puzzle always presents extra difficulties if any of the pieces are missing. The Hebrew tradition is the foundation of three major living religions and has been the basis of the spiritual life of the Western world for many centuries. The cycle of Hebrew myth (which has been beaten out into linear time and thinly disguised as history) is the underlying myth which can be related to other Semite, Egyptian and Greek myths, which together throw new light onto the Bronze Age.

Whereas it is impossible to invent a new myth, because myth is, of its nature, the distilled wisdom of the past which has left its trace or mark in the collective unconscious of the race, the same old myth may find new life once it is restored to its proper context in the Age of Myth. These deeper roots (from which Hindu and Nordic mythology do not seem to be excluded) could be better suited to the evolving psychological needs of the coming age with its more universal consciousness.

PART TWO

The Facts
Behind the Myth

The enduring myth, whether personal or collective, draws its material from many sources including facts. So far as the myth is concerned, facts are merely raw material, grist for the mill.

In the case of the Hebrew-speaking people, it would seem that the particular sequence of events which formed their history was most especially suited to their cycle of myth: they fitted the seasons of the year so neatly that they appear more symbolic than historical. But facts and history can be symbolic without necessarily having been reworked into legend.

Mythologically, the end of the year (whenever it comes) inevitably celebrates death and destruction, making way for the New Year, associated with the renewal of creation. In the case of West Semites, this new year was celebrated in the spring. The old year would have ended with the account of the Plagues and a ten day celebration of the destruction of every aspect of creation: the sun hides its light; water is polluted; vegetation, animals and men are all destroyed. This is followed by the Conquest in the same spring festival, and eating the fruits of a new land. The zenith of the year, high summer, has been associated with an enthronement festival, and for the Hebrew-speaking people their rise to power and consolidation of their empire. This is followed rapidly by their fall (in the Fall), their destruction at the hands of their neighbours, with the ensuing Dark Ages for them and their neighbours alike, down to the nadir of midwinter. At midwinter comes the other great turning point and the seeds of new beginnings, in the upturn of the year; this I associate with Joseph, supervising the supply of grain from the granaries in the winter months, before the devastation of the Plagues, and the beginning of another cycle.

This story begins with the tentative identification of Joseph with Imhotep, which is the first of four landmarks in the story. Of these landmarks, the Plagues and the Conquest stand together at the end of the Early Bronze Age (c. 2300 BC) to form the massive central twin pillars of the thesis. Joseph

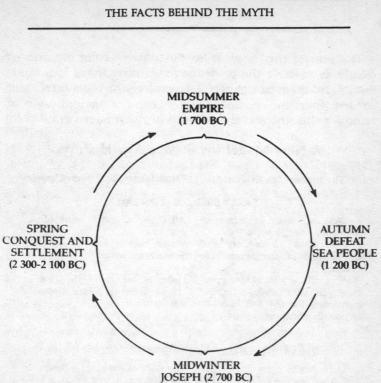

Fig. 1 *Symbolic Facts*
The history of the Hebrew-speaking people falls neatly into four
parts of approximately 500 years each that match the seasons of
the year in which that cycle of history was celebrated.

is but a flying buttress, as it were, four hundred years earlier;
if the hypothesis were not already on solid foundations, a
mere individual would fail to buttress it. On the other side,
four hundred years later, there is the great Hebrew-speaking
empire of the West Semites corresponding in general and in
detail to the empire of David and Solomon. The whole period
covers a thousand years and more.

The aim of this book is to put down as simply and as clearly as possible the evidence concerning these four landmarks and then, in Chapter 7, to explore the most important consequence: the relationship between the ancient myth of remote antiquity, and the religion of the modern era.

A New Model for Bronze Age History

The Bronze Age Evidence	Parallels from the Hebrew Chronicle

I. EARLY BRONZE (3300–2300 BC)

c. 2850 BC. Rise of Sumerian city-states. Semite *migrations*.	Abraham *migrates* from Mesopotamia.
c. 2700 BC. *Vizier Imhotep* and the Legend of the *Seven Year Famine*.	Vizier *Joseph* saves Egypt from *Seven Year Famine*.
Semites rule at least twelve provinces on *Nile Delta*. 'Habiru' mentioned for the first time in an outside document.	Hebrews are given the best of the land in the Delta and stay 400+ years.

II. EARLY-BRONZE/MIDDLE-BRONZE (2300–2100 BC)

Period of hiatus everywhere. Ipuwer describes the collapse of the Pyramid Age in *pollution, famine and plagues*. Half the population *leaves*.	The story of the *plagues* describes the ritual celebration of a time when Egypt was stricken with *pollution, famine and disease*. The time of the famous '*Exodus*'.
Sacred site at Har Karkom in *Sinai*, with *Temple and menhirs* – not used after this period.	Professor Anati identifies this site with *Mount Sinai*, where Moses found the prototype *Temple* and erected *pillars*.
Freak occupation of the *wilderness* of the Negev.	Hebrews spend forty years in the same *wilderness*.
Sargon founded the Empire of *Agade* which formed the *Eastern* bloc of Semite power.	*Moses* settled *Gad*, in its *Eastern* territories.
The massive *walls of Jericho* fell outwards and *nomads invaded*.	Processions with trumpets celebrate the *fall of the walls of Jericho*, when Joshua's army *invaded*.
Thick layers of ash reveal that *every city* in the Levant was *burned* in this period, including *Ai* which was never rebuilt.	Joshua's armies burn city after city, including *Ai*.

III. MIDDLE BRONZE (2100–1500 BC)

The hey-day of the Semites. Their tribal confederacy includes Palestine, Old Phoenicia and Syria, plus contacts with Mesopotamia.

Hebrews settle in the Levant. 'Period of the Judges' lasted *c.* 400 years.

West Semites use proto-Hebrew alphabet, Hebrew place-names, personal names, month names etc.

Hebrew culture reveals abundant parallels with the West-Semite culture of this period. There appears to be no break: they share the same burial customs, feasts, etc.

Tribal society changes to *feudal structure*, with first *King, Salitis.*

Similar changes with the consolidation of Hebrew power in the hands of the *Monarchy: Saul.* Saul was killed by an *arrow*. David organized *bowmen and chariotry* in his army.

'Asiatic Bow' and *chariot-warfare* are source of West Semite power.

Monumental building works, and *worldwide trade.*

Garrison cities built for the chariots. The *Kings of the Earth* pay *tribute* to Solomon.

IV. LATE BRONZE (1500–1200 BC)

Babylon and Avaris fall. Tuthmosis III sealed the fate of West Semites at *Megiddo.*

Is this Battle of *Megiddo* the source of the legendary *'Armageddon'*?

Sea Peoples sack cities from Troy to Tyre.

A scourge from the North will leave the Hebrews few in number.

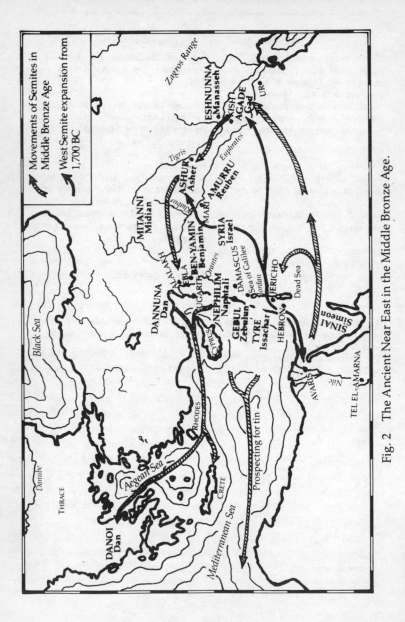

Fig. 2 The Ancient Near East in the Middle Bronze Age.

=== 2 ===

LORD OF DREAMS

Introducing the Parallels between Imhotep and Joseph

The reputations of gods and great men alike are apt to be whittled away by time. Few survive the process at all, and when they do it is usually only in reduced circumstances. Gods have been reduced to demons, then ogres in fairy tales and may end up as imps. The tattered remnants of ancient ritual appear as Halloween and bonfire night, or quaint dances round the maypole. Conjuring tricks and harlequins may be all that is left of the great magician gods who produced the world and divided day from night. The hermetically sealed jar may be the last memorial to Hermes and the secret mysteries of the Hermetic tradition.

People get bored easily. They don't want to hear about people they've never met, people who were dead before they were born, which makes it surprising if anyone survives this process, especially when they are still known by name centuries later, even thousands of years later. It suggests something of their stature, their influence.

Joseph is such a figure. His story is described with far more biographical detail than any of his ancestors. Many have searched the annals of Egyptian history hoping to find some corresponding figure, but none of the candidates so far have been truly convincing.

43

However, up till now, nobody has extended their search as far back as the Old Kingdom of Egypt. This is because they have placed such rigid faith in the overall chronology of the Hebrew chroniclers.

My reasons for looking back to the Pyramid Age have been outlined in Chapter 1. From the very start of my researches I took as my main anchor the Conquest, which of all the events in Hebrew history seemed likely to have left the clearest trace in the archaeological record. It was from this base, this platform, that I started looking for a figure corresponding to Joseph 400 years or so before that time.

Of course I wasn't particularly hopeful. Whereas a conquest could be expected to leave traces in the archaeological record, the chances of finding any corroboration of the story of Joseph seemed very slim. Even the story of a prominent individual, a vizier second in rank only to the king himself, is still only the story of a single man and hardly likely to survive nearly five thousand years. If you consider that we cannot yet establish the origin of the Sumerians in this same remote era, a whole race, with a particular contribution to architecture, art and literature, then it would be an extraordinary chance to be able to trace a particular individual in such a remote period of antiquity.

By just such a chance, a hundred years ago in 1889, a distinguished American Egyptologist, Mr C. E. Wilbour, accidentally discovered a faint inscription (which had escaped the notice of scores of travellers searching rocks for just such hieroglyphics) on a huge granite block on the island of Sehel.

Wallis Budge translated the text into English. It concerns a seven-year famine in the reign of King Djoser, and the advice of his vizier Imhotep. We know of this vizier from other inscriptions, and we have statuettes of him. He was one of the few individuals in the whole course of Egyptian history to be honoured with the rank of full deity – equal to the pharaohs themselves. His reputation was eclipsed only by the coming of Christianity three thousand years later and, even so, it was preserved among the alchemists. And recently interest in him has been slowly reviving. Jamieson Hurry has devoted a book to him and opens it by quoting Sir W. Osler: 'Imhotep is the first figure of a physician to stand out clearly from the mists of antiquity.' One of the few from remote antiquity to appear through those mists that continually wreathe and shroud the long dead.

In his introduction to the tale of the seven-year famine, Wallis Budge is struck by the resemblance to the story of Joseph. Indeed the parallels are striking. It isn't just that both stories concern a vizier who helps avert the dire consequences of a seven-year famine. Even the names of the viziers have something in common. Joseph's Egyptian name, Zaphentath-Paneah, was preserved in Hebrew tradition and may be a distortion of Zaphon-Imhotep.

In both stories the king has a dream about the Nile giving forth of its abundance.

In both stories there are concessions of land: in the Egyptian story twelve tracts of land on both sides of the river with all their revenues and taxes. In Joseph's story it is the best of the land in the Delta region of the Nile given to the twelve brothers, and their descendants.

In both stories tithes are collected.

Whereas Imhotep was master-builder of the first step pyramid, in popular tradition the first pyramids were long held to be the granaries built by Joseph.

Imhotep was identified with Asklepios, and in both cases their cult of healing depended chiefly on dreams and dream interpretation. Similarly the interpretation of dreams features prominently in the story of Joseph.

Imhotep was one of a handful of great wise men of Ancient Egypt, noted for his sayings which were treasured for many centuries but unfortunately have not survived. His great reputation was as a sage, an astronomer, a physician capable of seemingly miraculous cures and the architect of the first step pyramid. As counsellor and vizier to the king he long held the reputation of a man of foresight able to discern the future. Similarly, Joseph in the Hebrew story has a divining cup, by which he can discern the future; we know of an ancient Semite method of pouring water and oil into such a cup and reading the patterns that form. In recent times the value of such methods for tapping the reserves of the unconscious mind have been rediscovered as in the ink-blot test. Like Imhotep, Joseph is praised as being wiser than all the wise men of Egypt. And Joseph dreams of all the stars of heaven bowing to his star, which again takes on new significance in the light of the importance of astronomy in remote antiquity.

There are many small details which would go unnoticed unless you were looking for them, but each contributes one more small drop of steel that forges the link between these two figures: Imhotep and Joseph. When Moses marched East out of Egypt bearing the coffin of Joseph with him, his god revealed himself as the 'Lord, your healer', thus identifying himself with the healing gods of the ancient world. He also instructed Moses to make a bronze serpent raised on a pole or Tau cross, which was the symbol of the healing gods, especially Asklepios. But perhaps most important of all is the great healing cult of the West Semites centred at Gubna. Standing on the coast, halfway between Egypt and Greece, it was famous for its cures in the Bronze Age. It provides the likely stepping stone by which the cult of Imhotep at Edfu was carried in remote antiquity to Epidaurus where the cult of Asklepios flourished in classical antiquity.

The fact that a cult of dreams, along with its prophets, was suppressed in King Josiah's time obviously means that such a cult existed, and suggests that it had been a part of Hebrew tradition going back to Joseph's time. Furthermore, the fact that Josiah ordered the destruction of the bronze serpent on a pole that had been made by Moses and preserved in the Temple until then, would tend to confirm that this symbol of the healing gods common to other nations in the Bronze Age was also part of the original older Hebrew tradition.

Apart from such particular considerations, there is also the general feel of the two figures. Both Imhotep and Joseph are figures of sufficient stature for their reputations to have endured from their day to this. The prestige of one matches that of the other. Though supposing they are in reality the same figure it must be admitted that it is Joseph's reputation that has been belittled with time, possibly on account of the reaction against dreams and dream interpretations by the time Hebrew chroniclers added the finishing touches to the tale.

But whether they are the same or not is ultimately for you to assess, from the evidence laid out before you. Evidence collected piecemeal and only very recently in terms of the life span of human society. There has been so little time to assimilate and assess all the fragments that have been so suddenly gathered in the last century or so.

A Note on the Names: Imhotep, Zaphenath-Paneah/Joseph, and Asklepios

In this note my only aim is to show that the above names may not be so different as they appear at first glance. In the process of transliterating names from one language to another distortions occur, and most especially when transliterating a syllabic script, such as hieroglyphs or Semitic cuneiform into an alphabetic script, the earliest of which was the Sinaitic script using a proto-Hebrew alphabet, developed by the West Semites. As Hurry points out, 'Egyptian hieroglyphs, like most of the Semitic scripts, do not indicate vowels, nor indeed do they always accurately represent the consonantal skeleton. For these reasons there is no certainty how words were actually sounded, and a multiform transliteration, largely based on conjecture, has resulted'.

Imhotep. Hurry lists thirty variant renderings of this name by Egyptian scholars over a few decades. They include 'Aiemapt',

'Eimhatpou', 'Imopth', 'Iu-em-hept' and 'Ymhothphe'. He depicts the glyths and transliterates them himself as Ij-m-htp, and vocalizes this as Imhotep. Superficially it would relate this name to other such names as Ptah-hotep, Re-hotep, meaning 'the gods Ra, Ptah (and others) are satisfied (with the offerings), and this brings peace'. But 'Imhotep' is constructed differently and, as it stands, would mean 'He who comes in peace'. However, according to Clay, 'IM' was a Syrian god identical with Baal Saphon. There are also instances in Egyptian history where names have been altered slightly to eradicate the name of a deity no longer worshipped (e.g. in the cases of Akhenamun, changed to Akhenaten, and Thutankaten to Tutankhamun.) Similarly, the Hebrew scribes gave harmless but somewhat contrived meanings to names which had honoured gods who were not part of the current cult. In the light of the other parallels between Imhotep and Joseph, it seems possible that a minor alteration in the structure of the glyphs could have been introduced by scribes to disguise the Syrian deity and, therefore, foreign origin of the name.

Zaphenath-Paneah. Possibly (Zaphon) TH-P-N-H. The vowels weren't written in Old Hebrew, and the order of the consonants is not as important in Semitic languages as in our Western languages. Zaphon means 'North' and the name could be a corruption of 'Im-of-the-North-is satisfied'.

Joseph. Possibly Jo-Saphon, a disguised form of Baal-Saphon. Later editors of the Bible have frequently substituted a shortened form of Jahweh for Baal. All the other tribal names are found in Semite documents outside the Bible, with the one exception of 'Joseph'.

Asklepios (identified with Imhotep by the Greeks). This could be a corruption of Kheri-heb. In Egyptian there is no letter 'L' and so 'R' is frequently an equivalent. Imhotep's important function was as the Kheri-heb priest, responsible for the ceremony of the 'opening of the mouth'. Like Imhotep, Asklepios was credited with being able to raise the dead to life.

Imhotep and the Seven-Year Famine

The Egyptian text found inscribed on granite on the island of Sehel describes an event which took place in the reign of King Djoser of the Third Dynasty, which inaugurated the Old Kingdom of Egypt in around 2700 BC, and was also called the Pyramid Age. The event was a terrible famine which lasted seven years.

In a royal dispatch sent to the South, the Pharaoh wrote:

This is to inform thee that misery hath laid hold upon me, upon the great throne ... My heart is grievously afflicted ... because the Nile hath not come forth in my time to the height for seven years. Grain is very scarce, vegetables are lacking altogether, every kind of thing which men eat for their food hath ceased ...

The storehouses which should contain supplies are opened, there cometh forth therefrom nothing but wind ...

The child waileth, the young man draggeth his limbs along, and the hearts of the aged people are crushed with despair; their legs give way under them, and they sink to the ground, and their hands are laid upon their bodies [in pain]. ... The nobles are destitute of counsel ...

My mind hath remembered, going back to former time when I had an advocate to the time of the gods, and of the Ibis-God, and of the chief Kher-heb priest, Imhotep.

A great offering of bread-cakes, beer, geese, oxen, and beautiful things of all kinds was offered to the gods and goddesses who dwell in Abu. And I found the God standing in front of me ... I made prayer and supplication before him. Then he opened his eyes, and his heart was inclined towards me and his words were strong, 'I am Khnum, who fashioned thee ... I am he who created himself, . . . who came into being at the beginning, and I am the Nile, who riseth according to his will, in order to give health to him that laboureth for me . . . A lake of water hath been poured out for me which embraceth the field and provides life for every nose according to his embrace of the field-land, . . . I will make the Nile rise for thee, and no year shall he fail, and he shall spread himself out in rest upon every land. Green plants and herbs and trees shall bow beneath their produce. The goddess of the harvest shall be at the head of everything, and every product shall increase by hundreds of thousands . . . The people shall be filled, verily to their hearts' desire . . . Misery shall pass away and the emptiness of their store-houses of grain shall come to an end. The land of Egypt shall come to be a region of cultivated land, the districts shall be yellow with grain crops and the grain shall be goodly. And fertility shall come according to the desire for it, more than hath ever been before.

Then I woke up and my courage returned and was equal to my former despair.

On the advice of the learned Imhotep, Djoser presented Khnum with twelve measures of land on both banks of the river, good land for cultivation, together with property in the city, to the east and west sides, with gardens on the river front. The Pharaoh continued:

And of all the calves which are cast throughout the regions . . ., one tenth of their number shall be set apart as animals which are sealed for all the burnt offerings which are offered up daily . . . and by every man who snareth lions in the mountains, when these things enter the city, one tenth shall be demanded.

And, moreover, the gift of one tenth shall be levied upon the gold, ivory, ebony, spices, and upon woods and products of every kind whatsoever, which the

... Egyptians, and every person whatsoever shall bring in ...

And further, I will cause the masons, ... and the workers in metal, ... and the sculptors in stone, ... and handicraftsmen of every kind whatsoever ... and every worker in wood, ... to pay tithe upon all the natural products and also upon the hard stones ...

And there shall be an inspector ... Nothing thereof shall be withheld of all these things in order to deceive the scribes, and the revenue officers and the inspectors of the king ...

And ... the gold, and silver, and copper, and real (i.e. precious) stones, and the [other] things, which the metal-workers require for the House of Gold, and the sculptors of the images of the gods need in the making and repairing of them ... shall be exempted from tithing, and the workmen also.[1]

In spite of intensive searches by W. B. Emery and others, no tomb or mastaba of Imhotep has been found.

From the time of Imhotep, throughout the Old Kingdom of Egypt, there was an overseer of the two granaries, of upper and lower Egypt. And each Governor of a province was put in charge of reserves of grain and, on occasion, instructed to distribute grain to another province in short supply.

Joseph and the Seven-Year Famine

Pharaoh dreamed that he was standing by the Nile, and behold, there came up out of the Nile seven cows, sleek and fat, and they fed in the reed grass. And behold, seven other cows, gaunt and thin, came up out of the Nile after them, and stood by the other cows on the bank of the Nile. And the gaunt and thin cows ate up the seven sleek and fat cows. And Pharaoh awoke. And he fell asleep and dreamed a second time; and behold, seven ears of grain, plump and good, were growing on one stalk. And behold, after them sprouted seven ears, thin and blighted by the east wind. And the thin ears swallowed up the seven plump and full ears. And Pharaoh awoke, and behold, it was a dream. So in the morning his spirit was troubled; and he sent and called for all the magicians of Egypt and all its wise men; and Pharaoh told them his dream, but there was none who could interpret it to Pharaoh.

Then the chief butler remembered there had been a Hebrew in prison with him who had interpreted his dream. And the Pharaoh sent for Joseph and told him about his dream.

Then Joseph said to Pharaoh, 'The dream of Pharaoh is one; God has revealed to Pharaoh what he is about to do. The seven good cows are seven years and the seven good ears are seven years; the dream is one. The seven lean and gaunt cows that came up after them are seven years, and the seven empty ears blighted by the east wind are also seven years of famine. It is as I told Pharaoh, God has shown to Pharaoh what he is about to do. There will come seven years of great plenty throughout all the land of Egypt, but after them there will arise seven years of famine, and all the plenty will be forgotten in the land of Egypt; the famine will consume the land, and the plenty will be unknown in the land by reason of that famine which will follow for it will be very grievous. And the doubling of Pharaoh's dream means that the thing is fixed by God, and God will shortly bring it to pass. Now therefore let Pharaoh select a man discreet and wise, and set him over the land of Egypt. Let Pharaoh proceed to appoint overseers over the land, and take the fifth part of the produce of the land of Egypt during the seven plenteous years. And let them gather all the food of these good years that are coming, and lay up grain under the authority of the Pharaoh and let them keep it. That food shall be a reserve for the land against the seven years of famine which are to befall the land of Egypt, so that the land may not perish through the famine.

This proposal seemed good to Pharaoh and to all his servants. And Pharaoh said to his servants, 'Can we find such a man as this, in whom is the Spirit of God?' So Pharaoh said to Joseph, 'Since God has shown you all this, there is none so discreet and wise as you are; you shall be over my house and all my people shall order themselves as you command; only as regards the throne will I be greater than you.' And Pharaoh said to Joseph, 'Behold, I have set you over all the land of Egypt.' Then Pharaoh took his signet ring from his hand and put it on Joseph's hand, and arrayed him in garments of fine linen, and put a gold chain about his neck; and he made him to ride in his second chariot; and they cried before him. 'Bow the knee!'[2]

Pharaoh called Joseph's name Zaphenath-Paneah. During the seven years of plenty Joseph stored up grain in great abundance like the sand of the sea, until the stores were so great that they could not be measured. Then the famine became severe all over the earth. All the land of Egypt was famished and the people cried to Pharaoh for bread. Moreover people from other lands came to Egypt to buy grain.

When Jacob learned there was grain in Egypt he said to his sons: 'Go down and buy grain for us there that we may live, and not die.' Before the famine had reached its worst, Joseph sent word to his father Jacob, to let him know of all his splendour in Egypt: 'Thus says your son Joseph, God has made me Lord over all Egypt; come down to me, do not tarry.'

When Jacob was told his heart fainted for he did not believe them. But later his spirit revived, and he offered sacrifices to the God of his father. And God spoke to him in his dreams and said: 'I am God, the God of your father. Go down to Egypt for I will there make of you a great nation. And there Joseph's hand will close your eyes.' All the people of the house of Jacob came down to Egypt and they numbered seventy in all.

During the famine Joseph gathered up all the money. When all the money was spent, the Egyptians still came to Joseph for food. Joseph gave them food in exchange for horses, flocks, herds and asses.

The following year they came again and said: 'There is nothing left to us in the sight of my lord, but our bodies and our lands. Buy us and our land for food, and we with our land will be slaves to the Pharaoh.' So Joseph bought all the land of Egypt for the Pharaoh and said: 'Now here is seed for you, and you shall sow the land. At the harvest you shall give a fifth part to the Pharaoh, and four fifths shall be your own.'

So Joseph made a statute concerning the land of Egypt and it stands to this day: the Pharaoh should have a fifth. Only the land of the priests did not become the Pharaoh's, for the priests had a fixed allowance which the Pharaoh gave them. Therefore they did not sell their land.

Then Pharaoh said to Joseph: 'The land of Egypt is before you: settle your father and your brothers in the best of the land. You shall eat of the fat of the land.' So Joseph settled his father and his brothers and gave them a possession in the land of Egypt, in the best of the land, as the Pharaoh had commanded. So they lived in Egypt and gained possessions in it and were fruitful and multiplied. Jacob lived in the land of Egypt for seventeen years and when he died Joseph fell on his father and wept over him and kissed him.

According to the Hebrew account Joseph's coffin was carried out of Egypt four hundred years later.

In the Context of the Early Bronze Age

Taken out of context, it is not a matter of huge importance whether Joseph can be identified positively or not,
or whether he lived about 4,000 or 5,000 years ago. But
the context is important. Taken in this new context, the
Hebrew stories could throw light on the very beginnings
of civilization, the earliest of written records and the first
of cities.

If by 'civilization', we mean the story of city life, then
the beginning of the story is Jericho, the oldest city in the
world so far unearthed.

In 6000 BC Anati suggests that it had already started trading in the treasures of the Dead Sea like salt, sulphur and
bitumen. Salt was essential for preserving food, sulphur was
needed for making fire and bitumen was used for caulking
boats at the very beginning of the great seafaring adventure of mankind. Trade brought wealth to Jericho where
the inhabitants in the Early Bronze Age built remarkable
terraced gardens and irrigated them. Perhaps we have the
vestiges of an eye-witness account of them: 'Lot lifted up
his eyes, and saw that the Jordan valley was well watered
everywhere like the garden of the Lord, like the land of
Egypt . . .'3 Could he be talking about artificial irrigation
as in Egypt? Who were these early sophisticated men? We
cannot be sure, but what indications there are (without
any language or writing to go by) seem to relate them with,
rather than divide them from, the later inhabitants in the
Early Bronze Age, who were either Semite or Hamite.

Several questions spring to mind. For example, could these
earliest of civilized men have preserved an oral tradition
of the Pluvial Age in the Mediterranean, the last Ice Age
further north, a truly catastrophic period for mankind, and
is this the background for the seven-day celebration of a
universal flood, observed annually by the descendants of
the survivors?

The inhabitants of Jericho appear already to have revered

the sacred pillar, which was the central focus in Semite and Hamite cult later (i.e. the Djed column, the wooden asherah, etc.). To what extent would this be related to the standing stones south of Jerusalem which are thought to be the most ancient megaliths in the world? Symbolically all such stones and pillars are related to the universal pillar which joins heaven and earth, and is the means of man's ascent to the heavens. This suggests a connection between these stones and the standing stone set up by Jacob to celebrate the ladder which joins heaven and earth after his night of vigil spent wrestling with divine forces, in the manner of every subsequent yogi and shaman.

The Djed column in particular is associated with the cult of Osiris, a Semite god, but worshipped almost universally in later times as Adonai (Lord) to the Semites, and Adonis to the Greeks. When Wallis Budge was writing he could find no precedent for the elaborate burial customs of ancient Egyptian ritual. He assumed, therefore, that they were introduced into Egypt by some foreign and unidentified ingredient in the Egyptian population, which is still a possibility that cannot be dismissed. There is the extraordinary resemblance between the Egyptian and the Tibetan Books of the Dead yet to be accounted for, and the very real possibility that the Sumerians came from India, with their writing and their culture already developed. But so far there is no evidence from India (or anywhere else) of a developed civilization prior to that of Mesopotamia. Since Wallis Budge was writing, Woolley has excavated Ur and revealed the extraordinary burial customs there, and the more recent excavations at Jericho have revealed those extraordinary bejewelled plastered skulls which do suggest early prototypes of the later Egyptian customs.

One of the more remarkable Mesopotamian tombs contains the figure of Mes-kalam-dug, the Priest-King of Ur. I cannot help wondering if this might not be the tomb of the Great High Priest Melchizedek (all the consonants are there) whose name and line, have left such a profound mark in Christian myth, although he plays so small a part in the original Hebrew story. If Joseph was Imhotep, then the time is about right. The legends surrounding Abraham would have their background in the consolidation of the Sumerian City States, *c.* 2850 BC when it is reasonable to suppose that some of the original Semite population might have migrated, though there is no actual evidence of any friction between the indigenous Semites and the incoming Sumerians. Even the Sumerian king-lists depict the older inhabitants as Semite; the first kings, such as Gilgamesh, have Semite names. Perhaps they avoided friction by migrating north and west. And perhaps the great princely Semite patriarch left the Priest-King of Ur on good terms. It would have been a memorable parting that was commemorated ever after, and when it had been commemorated for some time in the city of Jerusalem (Ur-salem) it was remembered as if it had actually taken place there.

So much for a brief glance at the kind of shift in perspective of the period before Imhotep, if he is to be identified with the Hebrew Joseph. Concerning Joseph himself and the four hundred years between him and Moses there is a wealth of outside material, although the Bible itself says nothing.

Interim Section One

THE FIRST GAP
(2700–2300 BC)

The time that the Hebrew people dwelt in Egypt was four hundred and thirty years.

Then Joseph died, and all his brothers and all that generation. But the descendants of Israel (*Jacob*) were fruitful and increased greatly; they multiplied and grew exceedingly strong; so that the whole land was filled with them.[1]

The Bible says nothing more about these four hundred years, so there are four hundred years completely unaccounted for in the Hebrew story. But if the Semites who inhabited the Delta during the Pyramid Age, which lasted four hundred years, were Jacob's descendants, then we know quite a lot about them from other sources. They not only multiplied but they prospered.

Indeed the Old Kingdom of Egypt was one of the periods of the greatest stability and prosperity in the whole history of mankind. The prosperity of this Pyramid Age was centred at Memphis and On (later called Heliopolis). Everything we know about it is in accord with the backdrop of the story of Joseph. He married a daughter of a priest of On. It was a free epoch when other men of low rank reached the highest positions – not so later. We have paintings of this period which depict the continuity of Egyptian life in the next world, and which could serve as illustrations of Joseph's story – a butler pouring wine for the Pharaoh and whispering that he knew the man who could interpret his dream?

The following centuries were an era of high civilization, during which the great cities of the Delta contained predominantly Semite populations. These were large cities, some of them numbering 60,000 inhabitants and more, comparable to Elizabethan London. Indeed, D. M. Mackenzie compares Memphis to London from Bow to Chelsea and from the Thames to Hampstead.

Just as I see significance in the comparative stature of Imhotep and Joseph, so I would suggest that this degree of civilization and sophistication is the likely precondition for laying down the first chapter of a work of literature of outstanding quality: the Bible. More specifically, if the Hebrews were in Egypt during the Pyramid Age, then this would add weight to Piazzi Smyth's observations, such as his suggestion that the interior dimensions of the coffer in the Great Pyramid match the interior dimensions of the Ark of the Covenant constructed by Moses. He further suggests that this coffer is related to the English measure of 'a quarter' of wheat. Smyth describes the pyramid as a time-capsule of knowledge, including the standard weights and measures of all Europe, but also astronomical knowledge which was only being rediscovered in the nineteenth century. In the pyramids are pictures of the ocean-going vessels that have proved capable of crossing the Atlantic.

Just as the sixteenth century London with its seafaring trade provided the prosperous and cultured background for Shakespeare's genius, Memphis and On in the Old Kingdom of Egypt gave birth to an extraordinary burst of literary activity. This could explain the literary genius of the Hebrews, if this were the birthplace of their nation. Mesopotamian Semites, after four hundred years in Egypt, emerged as the distinct Hebrew-speaking people at the end of the Old Kingdom, when they are mentioned by name in Egyptian annals for the first time as 'The Hapiru'.

· They may already have been sailing to Europe. The word 'Europe' is thought to derive from a Semite word for west, and could be related to 'Hapiru' as well as Iberia and Britain. To the impartial mind, this first mention of 'The Hebrews' in an outside document is just as significant as the first mention of the 'People of Israel' a thousand years later.

═══ 3 ═══

PLAGUES AND CONQUEST

Introducing the Plagues

There was a great upheaval throughout the Ancient Near East at the end of the Early Bronze Age (*c.* 2300 BC). This marked the end of the Old Kingdom, or Pyramid Age, in Egypt, the eclipse of the Sumerians in Mesopotamia and the destruction of the Early Bronze Age civilization in the Levant. It was undoubtedly a time of terrible earthquakes, and there may have been some global catastrophe at the time, possibly involving a comet that orbited the earth too close for comfort.

This coincided with the end of the Age of Taurus, an earth sign in the Zodiac, and the beginning of the Age of Aries, a fire sign. It was a period of destruction and devastation which also involved large-scale migration of people: whole populations on the move.

From Egypt we have two vivid accounts of this period: the lament of the sage Ipuwer, and the papers of Nefer-rohu. Their stories bear a striking resemblance to the Hebrew story of the plagues in Egypt. Immanuel Velikovsky was the first to be struck by these parallels.

In both accounts a sage confronts the Pharaoh and lets him know the condition of the land and the people, as grief stalks a land of famine and pollution. In both stories there is oppression and insurrection. Both speak generally of disease, plague and freak storms. In particular, both the Hebrew and the Egyptian texts declare that the 'Nile is turned to blood'. In both there is dust and darkness. In both reptiles thrive at the expense of men, though the Egyptians speak of crocodiles while the Hebrews speak of frogs. In both accounts infants are killed, even the child of the Pharaoh. Translating the Egyptian, Adolph Erman suggests that half the population of Egypt left in the night. Finally, those who survive the catastrophe are commanded to celebrate their deliverance in a similar manner.

The Hebrew story is more a description of the annual ritual that preserved the race memory of these events, whereas the Egyptian texts seem closer to the events themselves. That is to say, the Hebrew account reads more like a ritual drama with the high priest intoning and the people responding. But in other respects even the superficial style of the accounts is similar. For example, the use of the word 'Behold' which comes like a refrain in both Egyptian and Hebrew versions. And both finish with 'Remember'.

I don't think anybody will fail to see the resemblance between the texts, and only somebody with a rigid pre-conceived idea about Hebrew chronology would want to deny that the Egyptian and Hebrew texts describe the same events. But you can judge for yourself from the following extracts.

The Egyptian Accounts of the Plagues: Ipuwer and Nefer-rohu

Then a sage, Ipuwer by name, appeared on the scene at court and told the whole truth. 'Behold, the mighty ones of the land, none reporteth to them the condition of the common people. Lies are told thee. I will speak of what is before me. What our ancestors have foretold is come.

All goeth to ruin.

It is grief that walketh through the land mingled with lamentations.

I show thee the land in lamentation and distress. That which never happened before hath happened.

Behold, the land is full of confederates. The stranger people from without are come into Egypt. The recruits whom we enrolled for us, are become a People of the Bow, ... and showeth the Bedouins the condition of the land.

Ah but had he perceived their nature in the first generation, then would he have smitten down evil; he would have stretched forth the arm against it, and destroyed the seed thereof and their inheritance ...

Oppression is on every side.

The hand reaches out with the stick ... They that were clad in fine linen are beaten ...

The Nile is in flood, yet none plougheth.

Nay, but they that build ... are become field-labourers, and they that were in god's bark are yoked together.

Nay but the officials are slain and their lists taken away.

Moreover hatred reigns among the townsmen ... Every town saith: 'Let us drive out the powerful from our midst.'

Behold no craftsman worketh; ... The washerman refuseth to carry his load.

Destroyed is the carrying out of that for which servants were sent on the behests of their lords. They say: 'Go ye upon the road which ye know.'

I show thee how the undermost is turned to uppermost.

All these years are confusion ... Would that thou mightest taste some of these miseries thyself!

Nay, but plunderers are everywhere ... Poor men now possess fine things.

Nay, but gold and lapis lazuli, silver and turquoise ... are hung about the necks of slave-girls.

Nay, but throughout the land insolence hath come to all men. The doorkeepers say: 'Let us go and plunder.'

Nay, but the hot-headed man saith: 'If I knew where God is, then would I make offering to Him.'

Nay, but they that were in the Pure Place [the dead lords], they are cast forth upon the high ground. The secret of the embalmers, it lieth open.

Nay, but magic spells are divulged and the secret of the kings is divulged.

Behold the kerehet snake is taken from its hole.

The whole land hath perished, there is nought left.

The land is left over to its weariness as when one hath pulled up the flax.

Corn hath perished everywhere ... Every one saith: 'There is no more.' The storehouse is bare, and he that kept it lieth stretched out on the ground ...

Nay, but men feed on herbs and drink water. No fruit nor herbs are longer found for the birds, and the offal is robbed from the mouth of the swine ...

The cattle rove about and there is none that careth for them. Each man fetcheth for himself therefrom and brandeth it with his name.

Nay, but the river is blood. Doth a man drink thereof, he rejecteth it as human, for one thirsteth for water.

Blood is everywhere.

Moreover, those good things are ruined, the fishponds ... which shone with fish and wild fowl.

Plague stalketh through the land.

Nay, but great and small say: 'I wish I were dead!'

Many dead men are buried in the river. The stream is a sepulchre. Nay, but the crocodiles are glutted with what they have carried off. Men go to them of their own accord.

Squalor is throughout the land. There is none whose clothes are white in these times. Nay, but men look like mudlarks.

How fareth this land?

The sun is veiled and will not shine that men may see. All men are dulled through want of it.

The sun separateth himself from men. None will know that it is midday, and his shadow will not be distinguished. None will live when the storm veileth it.

The sky hath still only the one wind.

They that had shade are in the full blast of the storm.

Nay, but gates, columns and walls are consumed with fire. Behold the fire will mount up on high.

Khnum fashioneth men no more because of the condition of the land.

Nay, but many women are barren.

Would that there might be an end of men, no conception, no birth.

Behold, ladies run. Their children are laid low in fear of death.

Nay, but the children of princes, men dash them against walls. The children that have been most earnestly desired, they are laid up on the high ground.

Khnum who fashioneth man is weary (of the waste).

There was once a man that was old and stood in the presence of death, and his son was still a child and without understanding, and opened not yet his mouth to speak unto you. Yet he was taken away through a deathly doom.

It is said: You are the herdsman of all men. You have spent the day in order to tend them. No evil is in your heart. Yet half your herd has departed in the night.

They have made tents for themselves like the barbarians.

A king shall come from the south, called Ameni. Be glad, ye people of his time!

It is good, however, when ships sail upstream again.

It is good, however, when the hands of men build pyramids and dig ponds, and make for the gods plantations with trees.

It is good, however, when rejoicing is in men's mouths and the magnates of districts look on, clad in fine raiment.

Remember how white bread is prepared on the day, and the offering-bread perpetuated.

Remember how oxen are slaughtered and fat geese laid on the fire (as offerings to the gods).

Remember how the regulations are observed and the days of the month adjusted.[2]

The Hebrew Account of the Plagues

In the Hebrew account, the plagues are recognized as the visitation from God, foretold by their ancestor Joseph.

The descendants of Israel were fruitful and increased greatly; they multiplied and grew exceedingly strong; so that the land was filled with them . . . [Pharaoh] said to his people, 'Behold, the people of Israel are too many and too mighty for us. Come, let us deal shrewdly with them, lest they multiply, and, if war befall us, they join our enemies and fight against us and escape from the land.'
. . . They set taskmasters over them to afflict them with heavy burdens, . . . The Egyptians were in dread of the people of Israel. So they made the people of Israel serve with rigour, and made their lives bitter with hard service, in mortar and brick, and in all kinds of work in the field.
Then the king of Egypt said to the Hebrew midwives, 'When you serve as midwife to the Hebrew women, and set them upon the birthstool, if it is a son you shall kill him . . .' But the midwives feared God and did not do as the king of Egypt commanded them . . .
Then Pharaoh commanded all his people, 'Every son that is born to the Hebrews you shall cast into the Nile . . .' . . .
One day when Moses had grown up, . . . he saw an Egyptian beating a Hebrew, one of his people. He looked this way and that, and seeing no one he killed the Egyptian and hid him in the sand . . .
In the course of those many days the king of Egypt died. And the people of Israel groaned under their bondage and cried out for help, and their cry under bondage came up to God . . .
Then the Lord said, 'I have seen the affliction of my people who are in Egypt, and have heard their cry

because of their taskmasters .. So I will stretch out my hand and smite Egypt with all the wonders which I shall do in it; after that he will let you go . . . and when you go you shall not go empty, but each woman shall ask of her neighbour, and of her who sojourns in her house, jewellery of silver and of gold, and clothing, and you shall put them on your sons and on your daughters; thus you shall despoil the Egyptians.'

Afterwards Moses and Aaron went to Pharaoh and said, 'Thus says the Lord, the God of Israel, "Let my people go, that they may hold a feast to me in the wilderness."'

But Pharaoh said, 'Who is the Lord, that I should heed his voice and let Israel go? I do not know the Lord, and moreover I will not let Israel go . . . Behold, the people of the land are now many and you make them rest from their burdens!' The same day Pharaoh commanded the taskmasters of the people and their foremen, 'Let heavier work be laid upon the men that they may labour at it and pay no regard to lying words.'

The foremen of the people went out and said to the people, 'Thus says Pharaoh, ". . . Go yourselves and get your straw wherever you can find it: but your work will not be lessened in the least."'. . .

Moses said to the Lord, 'Behold . . . how then shall Pharaoh listen to me?' And the Lord said to Moses, 'See I make you as God to Pharaoh . . . Go to Pharaoh in the morning, as he is going out to the water, . . . and you shall say to him, "Behold, I will strike the water that is in the Nile with the rod that is in my hand, and it shall be turned to blood, and the fish in the Nile shall die, and the Nile shall become foul, and the Egyptians will loathe to drink water from the Nile."'

Moses and Aaron did as the Lord commanded. In the sight of Pharaoh and in the sight of his servants, he lifted up the rod and struck the water that was in the Nile, and all the water that was in the Nile turned to blood. And the fish in the Nile died; and the Nile became foul, so that the Egyptians could not drink water from the Nile; and there was blood throughout all the land of Egypt ... And all the Egyptians dug round about the Nile for water to drink, for they could not drink the water of the Nile.

But the magicians of Egypt did the same by their secret arts; so Pharaoh's heart remained hardened, and he would not listen to them. Pharaoh turned and went into his house, and he did not lay even this to heart.

Then the Lord said to Moses, 'Go unto Pharaoh and say to him, "... Behold, I will plague all your country with frogs ..."'

And the frogs came up and covered the land of Egypt. [Pharaoh agreed to let the people go, and the Lord ended the plague of frogs] The frogs died out of the houses and courtyards and out of the fields. And they gathered them together in heaps and the land stank.

But when Pharaoh saw that there was a respite, he hardened his heart, and would not listen to them; as the Lord had said.

The Lord brought down other plagues on the Egyptians, of gnats and of flies, but Pharaoh remained hard. Moses returned to the court of the Pharaoh.

'Behold, the hand of the Lord will fall with a very severe plague upon your cattle which are in the field, the horses, the asses, the camels, the herds and the flocks.' All the cattle of the Egyptians died, but of the cattle of the people of Israel not one died ... But the heart of Pharaoh was hardened, and he did not let the people go.

And the Lord said to Moses, 'Take handfuls of ashes

from the kiln, and let Moses throw them toward heaven in the sight of Pharaoh. And it shall become fine dust over all the land of Egypt, and become boils breaking out in sores on man and beast throughout Egypt.' Moses threw them towards heaven, and it became boils breaking out in sores on man and beast.

Then the Lord said to Moses, '. . . say to him, "Thus says the Lord, the God of the Hebrews, Let my people go, that they may serve me. For this time I will send all my plagues upon your heart . . . I could have put forth my hand and struck you and your people with pestilence, and you would have been cut off from the earth . . . behold, tomorrow about this time I will cause a very heavy hail to fall, such as never has been in Egypt from the day it was founded until now. Now therefore send, get your cattle and all that you have in the field into safe shelter; for the hail shall come down upon every man and beast that is in the field and is not brought home, and they shall die."'

. . . The Lord sent thunder and hail, and fire ran down to the earth . . . there was hail and fire flashing continually in the midst of the hail such as had never been in all the land of Egypt since it became a nation . . . And the hail struck down every plant of the field, and shattered every tree of the field.

. . . And Pharaoh's servants said to him, 'Do you not yet understand that Egypt is ruined?'

So Moses stretched forth his rod over the land of Egypt, and the Lord brought an east wind upon the land all that day and all that night and when it was morning the east wind had brought the locusts . . . such a dense swarm of locusts as had never been before, nor ever shall be again for they covered the face of the whole land so that the land was darkened, and they ate all the plants in the land and all the fruit of the trees which the hail had left; not a green thing remained, neither tree nor plant of the field, through all the land of Egypt.

. . . Then the Lord said to Moses, 'Stretch out your hand toward heaven that there may be darkness over the land of Egypt, a darkness to be felt.'

So Moses stretched out his hand toward heaven and there was thick darkness in all the land of Egypt three days; they did not see one another, nor did any rise from his place for three days; but all the people of Israel had light where they dwelt . . .

The Lord said to Moses, 'Yet one plague more I will bring upon Pharaoh and upon Egypt . . .

'About midnight I will go forth in the midst of Egypt; and all the first-born in the land of Egypt shall die, from the first-born of Pharaoh who sits upon his throne, even to the first-born of the maidservant who is behind the mill; and all the first-born of the cattle. And there shall be a great cry throughout all the land of Egypt, such as there has never been, nor ever shall be again.' . . .

At midnight the Lord smote all the first-born in the land of Egypt from the first-born of Pharaoh who sat on his throne to the first-born of the captive who was in the dungeon and all the first-born of the cattle. And Pharaoh rose up in the night, he, and all his servants, and all the Egyptians; and there was a great cry in Egypt, for there was not a house where one was not dead . . .

And the Egyptians were urgent with the people, to send them out of the land in haste. The people of Israel had also done as Moses told them, for they had asked of the Egyptians jewellery of silver and of gold, and clothing; and the Lord had given the people favour in the sight of the Egyptians, so that they let them have what they asked. Thus they despoiled the Egyptians.

And the people of Israel journeyed from Rameses to Succoth, about six hundred thousand men on foot, besides women and children. A mixed multitude also went up with them, and very many cattle, both flocks and herds.

The Lord said to Moses and Aaron in the land of Egypt, 'This month shall be for you the beginning of months; it shall be the first month of the year for you ... on the fourteenth day of this month ... the whole assembly of the congregation of Israel shall kill their lambs in the evening ... They shall eat the flesh that night, roasted; with unleavened bread and bitter herbs they shall eat it. Do not eat any of it raw or boiled with water, but roasted, its head with its legs and its inner parts ... This day shall be for you a memorial day, and you shall keep it as a feast to the Lord; throughout your generations you shall observe it as an ordinance forever.'

And Moses said to the people, 'Remember this day ... When the Lord brings you into the land ... which he swore to your fathers to give you, a land flowing with milk and honey, you shall keep this service in this month ... at its appointed time from year to year.'[3]

Sargon and Moses

If Moses was involved in the collapse of the Pyramid Age in Egypt, then this would make him a contemporary of Sargon the Great. And the two figures have enough in common to make it tempting to compare them.

To begin with, it's their stature, their weight. They were both great figures who left their mark. You may not have heard of Sargon the Great, but that's only because this period of history has been somewhat neglected. He was one of the few great individuals who stand out in the 2,500 years of Bronze Age history. His name and his legend rang down the centuries. He was recognized as the founder-leader of all the Semite dynasties in Babylon and Assyria, right down into classical times when Sargon II of the Assyrian empire took his name 1,500 years later.

Like Moses, Sargon I had a reputation for not only making history but also for recording it. Unfortunately very little of his records survive unless, of course, he was Moses. Moses was recorded as having settled the tribe of 'Gad' in territories

71

east of the river, and there are reasons for supposing that these territories may have been east of the river Euphrates (see map on page 42). Sargon, on the other hand, founded the empire of 'Agade'.

So much for a few general similarities, but so far we have overlooked one important difference: the story of Sargon takes place in Mesopotamia while the story of Moses takes place in Egypt. But as in the case of Asklepios, I would suggest again that accurate geography was not the same obsession in the Age of Myth as it is today – and even today it is not of the same importance to the mythological mentality as it is to the logical mentality.

Each nation, and even each city, was inclined to adapt its heroes and its gods. If Moses ended his days in Agade, then in the course of time, the story of his legendary birth might all too easily have been transferred from the Nile to a more local river, where the annual celebrations might take place.

Here is the story of Sargon's birth:

> Sargon, strong king, king of Agade am I. My mother was a high priestess, my father I do not know. My paternal kin inhabit the mountain region.
>
> My city of birth is Azupiranu, which lies on the bank of the Euphrates. My mother, a high priestess, conceived me, in secret she bore me. She placed me in a reed basket, with bitumen she caulked my hatch. She abandoned me to the river from which I could not escape. The river carried me along; to Aqqi, the water drawer, it brought me. Aqqi, the water drawer, when immersing his bucket lifted me up. Aqqi, the water drawer, raised me as his adopted son. Aqqi, the water drawer, set me to his garden work. During my garden work, Ishtar loved me so that I ruled fifty-five years as king . . . from my city of Agade.[4]

The resemblance to the story of the birth of Moses has

not escaped notice. Brian Lewis, who translated the text, and Professor Anati are among the many who have noted it. There is also an Indian version of the story, but since the Empire of Agade had definite links with the Indus valley civilization, all three stories may still refer to the same founder of this ancient dynasty. Neither do the mythological associations preclude this possibility. The story can be associated with the coffin of Osiris floated in the Nile, with baskets in honour of Adonis and with Attis tied to bundles of twigs and set afloat, but all these stories would be associated with the priest-kings of the ancient world and would tend to confirm Moses' role as such a king: the Sun-king, the Roi-Soleil of remote antiquity with divine rights that made him 'as a God'.

The story of Moses' birth is as follows:

> Now a man from the house of Levi went and took to wife a daughter of Levi (*the hereditary priests*). The woman conceived and bore a son ... and when she could hide him no longer she took for him a basket made of bulrushes, and daubed it with bitumen and pitch; and she put the child in it and placed it among the reeds at the river's brink ... Now the daughter of Pharaoh came down to bathe at the river, and her maidens walked beside the river; she saw the basket among the reeds and sent her maid to fetch it: when she opened it she saw the child; ... and he became her son; and she named him Moses for she said, 'Because I drew him out of the water.'[5]

There is some tenuous evidence to suggest that Sargon or his dynasty had played a part in the collapse of the Old Kingdom of Egypt. Perhaps more significant are Moses' early connections with the Midian: he is away in Midian for a considerable time and married the daughter of Jethro the Midianite priest. If 'Midian' is the Hebrew rendering of 'Mitanni' then this suggests a connection with the

Upper Euphrates where the important Mitanni people were based.

We don't have very much direct evidence about the life of Sargon, but there is one other text which deserves consideration here, because it concerns a period Sargon spent in the wilderness. The short text is badly damaged, and what is left of it contains nothing resembling the exploits of Moses in the wilderness, apart from the bare fact that Sargon, too, was associated in legend with a period in the wilderness. Nevertheless I give Brian Lewis's translation in full, partly to show how fragmentary the evidence often is; the complete picture can only be gleaned from such evidence slowly, and much of the evidence has only recently come to light, which is why there is room for a radical re-appraisal.

> To . . .
> . . . and the huqu-bird . . . and the ewe ran about in the steppe, why not . . . and the gazelle, the . . . of the wind, the stag . . . The qata-bird was crying out in its continuous crying, what did it achieve? The wind blew . . . The wild ass ran about, he spent the night in the steppeland. . . . a swift onager . . . The wolf did not escape the blood . . . The devouring lion . . . the spiller of blood . . . the smearer of blood . . . It ran about from the judgement of Samash . . . The wind blew the house of men. . . . the temple of . . . . . . turns into wasteland.[6]

More important are Professor Anati's archaeological discoveries in the Sinai desert. In his recent work, *The Mountain of God*, he describes finding a mountain in the Sinai peninsular which had long been a site of worship. Furthermore there were twelve menhirs, or standing stones, at the base of the mountain which fitted the description in the Hebrew Chronicle of how Moses 'rose early in the morning and built an altar at the foot of the mountain, and twelve pillars, according to the twelve tribes of Israel.'[7] And on top of the mountain there was also a small temple which fitted the biblical description of the model of a temple shown to Moses on the mountain.

Anati identifies this mountain with Mount Sinai, but it was a place of worship only up to the end of the Early Bronze Age and not later. If this was the Sinai where the ten commandments were given to Moses, then in Anati's words there was 'a discrepancy of almost 1,000 years', 'the history of the Hebrew people is suddenly increased by approximately 1,000 years', because 'the revelation on Mount Sinai now dates back to the third millennium BC.'[8]

In this context we may note that the laws formulated for Moses on the mountain closely resemble laws already prescribed by Ptah-hotep and Merikare in the Pyramid Age in Egypt. For example:

1 Revere the God.
2 Copy thy father; them that have gone before thee.
3 Expel no man from the possessions of his father.
4 Slaughter not, that doth not profit thee.
5 Oppress no widow. Be not covetous. Beware of covetousness.
6 Do right so long as thou abidest on the earth.

7 Exalt not the son of one of high degree more than him that is of lowly birth.
8 If thou be grown great after that thou wast of small account, and have gotten thee substance, after that thou wast aforetime needy in the city which thou knowest, forget not how it fared with thee in time past. Trust not in thy riches that have accrued to thee as a gift of God.[9]

Professor Anati acknowledges that his 'conclusion naturally requires a revision of the entire chronology of events presented in the biblical narrative.'

Similarly, Professor Cohen has examined traces of a freak occupation of the Negeb around the end of the Early Bronze Age. These traces were first described by Nelson Glueck, but in his article for the *Biblical Archaeology Review*, Cohen produces his evidence for thinking that these people had come out of Egypt and suggests that these 'mysterious people who migrated from Egypt into the Central Negeb at the turning point between the Early and Middle Bronze Age may be the Israelites whose famous journey from Egypt to Canaan is called the "Exodus". Such an identification should not be ruled out.'[10]

This period is sometimes called the 'First Intermediate Period'. It was a period of great upheaval, of shifting populations. From the archaeological record alone, it is certain that a vast horde settled in a region that had never been inhabited before and was virtually uninhabitable. But why? The biblical narrative may provide clues. It describes a fire of the Lord that consumes 250 men, a time when the sun stood still for nine days, and fiery serpents, which are consistent with meteorites dropping from the tail of a comet orbiting the earth too close. The only way the sun could stand still in the sky for nine days would be if the earth had been knocked from its vertical axis and continued to spin, but with the northern hemisphere facing the sun and southern hemisphere in darkness, and then righted itself.

Whatever the case, there were certainly fearsome earthquakes at this time. The biblical narrative describes how:

> the ground under them split asunder; and the earth opened its mouth and swallowed them up, with their households and all the men that belonged to Koran and all their goods. So that they and all that belonged to them went down alive into Sheol; and the earth closed over them, and they perished from the midst of the assembly. And all Israel that were round about them fled at their cry; for they said, 'Lest the earth swallow us up!'[11]

And Kathleen Kenyon's excavation at Jericho tells a similar tale: a series of successive earthquakes at the end of the Early Bronze Age – culminating in the final disaster for that city.

The Conquest

Set in the context of the destruction of the magnificent ancient civilization which had flourished in the Levant throughout the Early Bronze Age, the Hebrew Chronicle of the events becomes vivid – not to say lurid.

By this time (*c.* 2300 BC), the whole of the Levant was covered with great walled cities which governed small surrounding city states, as if the oldest city in the world, Jericho, had had many offspring in the intervening four thousand years, and its offspring had spread across the area. These cities stretched east across the Jordan and Dead Sea into the area that would later be called Edom, and also west as far as the other salt sea, the Mediterranean, where there were the great ports of Sidon and Gubna on the coastal plain, which were already shipping cedarwood from the Lebanon mountains to Egypt.

The houses within the cities were of wood which was plentiful throughout the area at that time. But the city walls were of brick and the foundations of many of them are there to this day. The excessive thickness of these walls at the base suggested to Kathleen Kenyon that they must have been extremely high.

When Moses sent out spies to Canaan, they returned with a cluster of grapes strung on a pole between two men, as well as pomegranates and figs. They reported:

We came to the land to which you sent us; it flows with milk and honey and this is its fruit. Yet the people who dwell in the land are strong, and the cities are fortified and very large; . . . And there we saw the Nephilim (the sons of Anak, who come from the Nephilim); . . . and we seemed to ourselves like grasshoppers, and so we seemed to them.[12]

Jericho itself, which lies deep below sea level in the Jordan rift, had been destroyed by earthquakes several times in fairly quick succession. Each time the inhabitants had rebuilt the walls thicker, no doubt in the hope that they would withstand the next earthquake. The final wall which they built was the most impressive of all. It was massive and built with extra large bricks, but to no avail. It fell outwards in another earthquake.

From the archaeological account alone, it is quite clear that the inhabitants could not rebuild it again because they were massacred by invading nomads, and their city was burned. But, curiously, there was some attempt to re-erect some kind of a wall, but it was done in a very different, higgledypiggledy style. Kenyon suggests that either the old inhabitants made this attempt in great haste, or else it was the newcomers trying their hand at bricklaying.

In the Hebrew description, 'the city and all that is within it shall be devoted to the Lord for destruction. The people went up into the city, every man straight before him and they took the city. Then they utterly destroyed all in the city, both men and women, young and old, oxen, sheep and asses with the edge of the sword ... And they burned the city with fire.'[13]

The nearby tombs of the nomadic invaders tell us quite a lot about them. They disposed of their dead with care. The largest type of tomb which Kenyon calls 'Outsize Type' involved removing one hundred and fifty tons of rock. She suggests that they resemble Egyptian hillside tombs (anticipating those in the Valley of Kings later) except that there were no images of gods in them. The picture that emerges is of a people who returned to the site to bury their dead properly. They probably followed a Semite custom of initially burying the dead in shallow graves, and later carrying the bones to ancestral burying grounds. Kenyon found five distinctive patterns of burial, 'which can be best explained as a number of tribal groups, each with its own burial customs, coming together as a loose tribal confederacy.' At these reunions, 'they must have lived in tents, which provides clear evidence of their nomadic origins.' And their broken pottery still lies in the ditches around Jericho.

I have kept back the description of the way in which the walls of Jericho fell until now, because it seems obvious to

78

me that it is a description of a great annual ceremony to celebrate the original event.

> The people came up out of the Jordan on the tenth day of the first month ... and those twelve stones which they took out of the Jordan, Joshua set up in Gilgal. And he said to the people of Israel, 'When your children ask their fathers in time to come, "What do these stones mean?" then you shall let your children know, Israel passed over this Jordan on dry ground. . . .'
> So Joshua made flint knives, and circumcised the people of Israel because they had not been circumcised on the way.
> When the circumcising of all the nation was done, they remained in their places in the camp till they were healed ... they kept the passover on the fourteenth day of the month.
> And on the morrow after the passover, on that very day, they ate of the produce of the land ...
> And as Joshua had commanded the people, the seven priests bearing the seven trumpets of ram's horns before the Lord went forward, blowing the trumpets, with the ark of the covenant of the Lord following them ...
> And the second day they marched around the city once, and returned into the camp. So they did for six days.
> On the seventh day they rose early at the dawn of day, and marched around the city in the same manner seven times ... And at the seventh time, when the priests had blown the trumpets, Joshua said to the people, 'Shout; for the Lord has given you the city ...' ... As soon as the people heard the sound of the trumpet, the people raised a great shout, the wall fell down flat.[14]

The trumpets were presumably used to simulate the way the earth groans before an earthquake. I think the make-shift wall, erected so carelessly, could have been used for dramatic effect, and was built up only in order to be pushed over at this point in the ceremony. I am certainly inclined to think that the crossing of the Jordan was not a separate event but a celebration of the earlier crossing of the Red Sea, and served to illustrate the process by which events came to be associated with local places in the course of cultic celebrations, and gradually became myth. Even though Kenyon doesn't connect this invasion with the Hebrew conquest, which she presumes took place a thousand years later, she still infers from the archaeological evidence that Jericho was the 'point of entry' for this invasion, which next captured and burned the city of Ai.

In the Hebrew account, after they had slaughtered the inhabitants of Ai, 'Joshua burned Ai, and made it for ever a heap of ruins, as it is to this day. And he hanged the king of Ai on a tree . . .'[15]

Every city so far investigated by archaeologists reveals a layer of ash at this level, indicating that it was burned down at the end of the Early Bronze Age. Kenyon suggests the invasion took place in two waves over quite a long period. The first wave penetrated from the south via Jericho and the second wave was from the east across Syria and the northern Levant. In the Hebrew chronicle Joshua also defeats the whole land, slaughtering the inhabitants and burning their cities, and hanging their kings from trees.

Towards the end of the account, there is particular mention of the part played by the eastern tribes of Gad, Reuben and Manasseh. Joshua sent them back to their homes in the east with their share of the booty as a reward for their help in the conquest. Only one of them is awarded any territory in the west. But before they crossed the Jordan they built an altar 'of tremendous size' at the frontier. It was a scandal, and when the people of Israel heard of it they gathered to make war against them. An altar of ordinary size is described in Ezekiel as stepped, like a small ziggurat, so an 'altar of tremendous size' would have been a ziggurat. This would seem to connect these eastern tribes with Mesopotamia where all the ziggurats were built. (Another connection is the giant bed of Og in their territory, as a bed of similar dimensions is associated with Babylon.)

From the archaeological record it appears that it was a considerable time, perhaps a century or so, before the newcomers started to settle and rebuild. And Kenyon suggests that this rebuilding could have originated from Gubna, on the coast.

This is interesting in the light of the Hebrew story concerning 'Gibeon', a place which cannot be located with any certainty. The people of Gibeon dressed up and pretended to be strangers from a distant land in order to make an alliance with Joshua. They promised to become his servants, so their lives were spared and they became the hewers of wood (the builders?) and the drawers of water for the Hebrews.

Certainly the inhabitants of the coastal plain, where Gubna was situated, were used as smiths and craftsmen until the reign of Solomon.

A Note on Two Waves of the Invasion

From the archaeological evidence alone it has been impossible to decide whether the nomads who conquered the Levant via Jericho in 2300 BC were the same as the Hebrew-speaking peoples who settled the land from 2100 BC.

The nomads who invaded were plainly there for about 200 years, living their nomadic lifestyle and returning to bury their dead in the tombs near Jericho. But around 2100 BC there were big changes. In particular, a huge rebuilding programme got under way, which K. Kenyon thinks was instigated from Gubna. There seem to have been two waves to the invasion and settlement, with minor discernible differences between the southern prong of the attack that entered via Jericho, and the northern prong. The northern prong appears to have been more related to the cultures of Syria and Mesopotamia.

If you take this evidence in conjunction with that of the Hebrew chroniclers, it seems this northern wave of attack could be associated with the part the eastern tribes played in the conquest, which is oversimplified in the Hebrew account. I think the eastern tribes may have returned in another wave when the Sumerians re-established their power on the Euphrates with the dynasty of Ur III (in 2100 BC).

Further, I think there may be a connection between the northern tribes, especially Ephraim and the Rephaim which was the Hebrew name for the old inhabitants of the land. They had not been exterminated at Gubna, nor to the east, in Old Assyria. As the conquered and oppressed previous inhabitants they were called the 'Rephaim', but when later assimilated into the Semite confederacy, perhaps they became the people of 'Ephraim'.

Interim Section Two

THE SECOND GAP
(2100–1700 BC)

> In the four hundred and eightieth year after the people
> of Israel came out of the land of Egypt, in the fourth
> year of Solomon's reign over Israel ... he began to
> build the house of the Lord.[1]

In the Hebrew chronicle, after the very detailed account
of the plagues and the conquest, there is a period of nearly
400 years which is hardly described at all. Four hundred
years are packed into the twenty-odd pages of one short
book, *The Book of Judges*. In this book, there is very little
historical detail of a kind that might leave a trace in the
archaeological record, or which could be corroborated or
refuted from outside documents. Most of it is taken up
with material that finds parallels in Bronze Age myth, not
history. For example, the Song of Deborah, which could
be compared with a hymn to the warlike Semite goddess
Dibborah, the wailing for Jephtah's daughter who is to be
sacrificed in a manner not unlike Iphigenia, and the long
and colourful story of Samson who has been compared to
Gilgamesh and Hercules – like Hercules he starts by slaying
the lion, and he ends up enslaved by Delilah, as Hercules
is enslaved by Omphale.

83

If the Hebrew account of the plagues and the conquest corresponds to the collapse of the Pyramid Age in Egypt and the nomadic invasion of the Levant that followed shortly after, then we can shed a little extra light on these 400 years from the archaeological data and outside documents. This is the period during which the West Semites settled the Levant. The general picture is of a loose federation of Semite powers throughout Western Asia, governed by 'Ensi', which has been translated as 'Judges'. The names of the different Semite powers, as well as the names of cities and individuals, are all familiar from the Bible. As John Bright points out, the names of all the Hebrew tribes are found in the context of the Middle Bronze Age with the exception of 'Joseph'. Some are mentioned in Egyptian curses, others are mentioned in the correspondence discovered at Mari.

But perhaps the most important evidence from this period are the fragments of Sinaitic script, fragments of a proto-Hebrew alphabet found at Gezer and in Sinai which still shows marked signs of its derivations from Egyptian hieroglyphs. Hebrew was being written as well as spoken by the West Semites of the Levant, who were sufficiently familiar with the complexities of Egyptian hieroglyphs to adapt them into an alphabet for the first time. This alphabet was later adopted by the Old Phoenicians, from there carried to Greece, and used worldwide.

4

THE RISE AND FALL OF THE HEBREW-SPEAKING EMPIRE

Just as I looked for a figure corresponding to Joseph about 400 years before the walls of Jericho fell and was surprised and delighted to find Imhotep, so in the case of the empire of Solomon and David I started looking for something in the archaeological record corresponding to an empire. In contrast with a mere individual, I certainly expected to find traces of this empire. If Joseph was Imhotep who inaugurated the Pyramid Age in Egypt, if the ritualized account of the Plagues corresponded to the collapse of the Old Kingdom, and if the Hebrews were the nomadic invaders who destroyed the Early Bronze civilization in the Levant, then about 400 years later, according to their own account, these same people consolidated their power, carried out some fairly massive building work and accumulated great wealth; some evidence of all this must have survived.

And sure enough, it was there, rather more extensive and grander than the chroniclers' description of it. The chroniclers, putting together their story 1,000 years later, also seem to have lost track of the 200 years' hiatus between the Early Bronze Age and the Middle Bronze Age, before the invaders began to settle. But 400 years after the beginning of the settlement (2100 BC) the West Semites did found an empire which was mighty and short lived, and which corresponds in many ways to the descriptions in the Hebrew account.

85

The Consolidation of Semite Powers Manifest in the Fortress Cities across the Near East

For a short period of not more than 200 years (*c.* 1700–1500 BC), the West Semites appear to have ruled all the important centres of the Ancient World. One of the most renowned figures among them was the founder-ruler of the first dynasty of Babylon, 'Hammurabi', whose name means 'Father of the West Semites'. His son and successor was Samsu-ilanu.

Asshur, or Old Assyria, was governed at this time by Shamshi Adad and a West Semite dynasty. Egypt was ruled by foreign kings (the 'Hyksos') and according to a later Egyptian historian Manetho, the first king among them was Salitis. One of his successors was Khyan, whose name has been found in Crete and beyond the Tigris. In his study of these foreign kings, J. van Seters has shown that their reign over Egypt was not as terrible as it was described later by the Egyptian historian. And an earlier account reveals that one of them built a temple of 'fair and everlasting work', in his city of Avaris. When these foreigners were driven out of Egypt, according to Manetho, they went up and founded Jerusalem, and the most ancient parts of the terrace walls around Jerusalem, the so-called 'Millo', date from the end of this period.

Whether these foreign kings used Avaris as their capital city or only as a summer residence is not certain, but either way the centre of their power remained the Levant and Old Phoenicia, their homeland. There they built fortress cities right across the country, usually built on mounds, with plastered slopes which are presumed to have been a defence against battering-rams and siege towers. Many of these were on a vast scale, the likes of which were never seen in the Levant earlier or later. They would seem to lie scattered along the strategic routes between the Nile and the Euphrates, from Gezer to Megiddo and north to Hazor, the greatest of all their cities.

We cannot be sure of the extent of the West Semite empire

at this time. We cannot know the exact relationship between the foreign rulers in Egypt and the builders of the fortress cities in the Levant and the contemporary rulers of Babylon and Old Assyria. But that is not important from the point of view of this study, for which it is the overall picture, the bird's-eye view that really matters. The central twin pillars of this overall picture are the plague-ridden land of Egypt at the end of the Old Kingdom followed by the nomadic invasion of the Levant, with its point of entry at Jericho. If these twin pillars need buttressing at all, then the story of Imhotep and the seven-year famine would seem to provide just such a buttress from the earlier period. But even more so, a West Semite empire 400 years later, whatever its formation or extent, would seem to provide a very substantial buttress from the later period. According to the Hebrew chronicle Saul, David, Solomon and Jeroboam founded a great empire with a centralized government and a huge programme of building activity.

With regard to the overall picture, here are the Egyptian accounts of Manetho (as quoted in Josephus) and of Ahmose, followed by the Hebrew parallel from Isaiah.

This is Manetho's description of the events.

> For what cause I know not, a blast of God smote us, and unexpectedly from the regions of the East invaders of obscure race marched in confidence of victory against our land. By main force they easily seized it without striking a blow; and having overpowered the rulers of the land, they then burned our cities ruthlessly, razed to the ground the temples of the Gods, and treated all the natives with a cruel hostility, massacring some and leading into slavery the wives and children of others. Finally, they appointed as king one of their number whose name was Salitis. He had his seat at Memphis, levying tribute from Upper and Lower Egypt, and always leaving garrisons behind in the most advantageous places.

... He founded a city very favourably situated on the east of the Bubastite branch of the Nile, and called it Avaris after an ancient religious tradition. This place he rebuilt and fortified with massive walls, ... and a garrison of two hundred and forty thousand armed men whom he put into it to keep it. Thither Salitis came in summertime, partly to gather his corn, and pay his soldiers their wages, and partly to exercise his armed men, and thereby to terrify foreigners. When this man had reigned thirteen years, after him reigned another ... And the first rulers among them ... were all along making war with the Egyptians, and were very desirous gradually to destroy them to the very roots. This whole nation was styled Hyksos, that is *Shepherd-Kings* ... but some say these people were Arabians.[1]

Manetho next describes the fall of Avaris, but his account (written centuries later) conflicts with the eye-witness story found in the tomb of Ahmose, son of Ebana:

I took service as a soldier in the ship of 'The Wild Bull' when I was a youth, and had not taken a wife, but spent my nights in a hammock of net.

Now when I had established a household, I was taken upon the ship 'Northern', because I was valiant; and I used to accompany the Sovereign upon foot in the course of his goings abroad in his chariot. And when they sat down before the town of Avaris, I displayed valour on foot in His Majesty's presence. Hereupon I was promoted to the 'Manifestation in Memphis'.

And when they proceeded to fight on the water in [the canal?] Pzedku of Avaris, I made a capture and brought away a hand, and it was reported to the King's informant, and the gold of valour was given to me.

Fighting was repeated in this place and I proceeded to make a second capture there and brought away a hand. And the gold of valour was given to me over again.

And when they fought in the [part of] Egypt south of this town [i.e. Avaris], I brought away a male living prisoner. I went down into the water – [for] he was taken prisoner on the city side – and carried him over the water with me. It was reported to the King's informant, and thereupon, behold, I was rewarded with gold afresh.

Then they proceeded to spoil Avaris; and I brought away spoil thence: one man; three women; a total of four heads. And his majesty gave them to me for slaves.[2]

And that is all he has to say about the matter. As Gunn and Gardiner comment: 'It is typical of the Egyptian indifference to bald facts that the only contemporary record that we possess of the taking of Avaris, a historic event of capital importance should be the biography of a naval officer on the walls of his tomb in a remote provincial town.'[3]

For the more general picture we still have to rely on Manetho who states that the defeated Hyksos, when they fled from Egypt, 'built a city in the country which is now named Judaea and called it Jerusalem.' And the terraced ramparts there originated in this period.

In particular Manetho's description of the arrival of the Hyksos in Egypt has parallels with one of the oracles collected in the Book of Isaiah (though it must be admitted that the Hebrew chroniclers also display a certain amount of 'indifference to bald facts' in this instance).

In that day the Egyptians will be like women, and tremble with fear before the hand which the Lord of hosts shakes over them. And the land of Judah will become a terror to the Egyptians; everyone to whom it is mentioned will fear because of the purpose which the Lord of hosts has purposed against them.

In that day there will be five cities in the land of Egypt which speak the language of Canaan and swear allegiance to the Lord of hosts. One of these will be called the City of the Sun . . .

And the Lord will smite Egypt, smiting and healing, and they will return to the Lord, and he will heed their supplication and heal them.

In that day there will be a highway from Egypt to Assyria, and the Assyrian will come into Egypt, and the Egyptian into Assyria, and the Egyptians will worship with the Assyrians.

In that day Israel will be the third with Egypt and Assyria, a blessing in the midst of the earth, . . .[4]

But perhaps it is time to consider and compare more substantial evidence, like the Hyksos cities that have been excavated, compared with the lists of cities built by David, Solomon and Jeroboam. Cities don't disappear without leaving some trace in the archaeological record. The Hebrew chroniclers describe in some detail the colossal building projects of the period. Gangs of forced labour were employed to build store cities and cities for the chariots and horsemen of the king. So, for example 'David put garrisons in Syria of Damascus'. Solomon had 550 officers in charge of the levy of slaves working on his projects to build the chariot cities with stalls for his 40,000 horses in all the kingdoms that he governed from the Euphrates to the border of Egypt. The Hyksos never ruled beyond Gebelen and to the south of that, Upper Egypt remained independent, though it paid tribute. Jeroboam is also credited with vast-scale building activities which is understandable if he ruled just when the West Semite empire was crumbling round him, and the neighbouring powers were gathering strength.

By far the majority of the distinctive Hyksos fortress cities that have been excavated so far are also mentioned in the Hebrew account of this period, and most of them were specifically fortified by David, Solomon or Jeroboam. Others are mentioned only as prominent cities at the time.

Below is a list of fortified Hyksos towns, which were also Hebrew garrisons, store cities or chariot cities at the time of the empire.

Bethel	Gubna (Gibeon)	Jerusalem
Beth-Shemesh	Hazor	Kadesh
Beth Sur	Hebron	Lachish
Damascus	Joppa	Megiddo
Dothan	Jericho (City	Shechem
Gath	of Palms)	Taanach
Gezer		

Hyksos towns not mentioned in the Hebrew chronicle are: Ashkelon, Avaris, Beth, Eglaim, Debir, Laish, Quatna and Sharuren. The Hebrew chroniclers also mention among the massive programme of building works Abel-Meholah, Adoraim, Adullam, Aijalon, Azeka, Baalath, Beth Horon, Bethlehem, Beth-shean, Elonbeth-hanan, Ekron, Etam, Makaz, Mareshah, Shaalbim, Socho, Tadmor, Tamar, Tekoa, Ziph and Zorah, as well as sixty great cities in Gilead/Argob, cities for chariots and horses in Lebanon, cities given by the King of Tyre, and store cities in Hamath.

But the important point from the two lists is the general picture that is created of great fortified cities across the land that lasted only a few generations but which would be remembered long after from the crumbling ruins and the great stones of the cyclopean masonry of the era. Stones that were still being reused in some cases nearly 1,000 years later. It is not easy to forget such a time of splendour when it is made manifest in huge stones and colossal building programmes.

The Chariot, the Bow, the Wealth and the Trade

The Chariot
The chariot, and the domesticated horse used to draw it, are

thought to have been introduced into the Ancient Near East by the Mitanni, who spoke an Indo-European language and were the aristocratic rulers of the Hurrian population on the Upper Euphrates.

But it was the West Semites who popularized their use. The fortress garrisons along the routes across the Levant must have served as posthouses where the horses could be changed, enabling much speedier communications throughout their territories. There can be little doubt that this newly developed war chariot was the means by which the West Semites consolidated their power in Western Asia and further afield. It was they who introduced the war chariot to Egypt. And if it was like the ones used by the Pharaohs soon after, then it was a light two-wheeled affair drawn by one or two horses, and capable of considerable speed as well as being highly manœuvrable.

The population of the West Semite invaders of Egypt was very mixed, as was the population of Western Asia at the time, especially the ports. As Kathleen Kenyon says in her *Archaeology of the Holy Land*: 'The ethnic ingredients of the Hyksos accords well with what we know about the Habiru (Hebrews).'5

In the *Books of Samuel*, which are extraordinarily detailed, there are two stories which throw light on the question of chariots. In the Bronze Age the chariots would have been made of bronze, and the first story is about metal workers. Unlike iron, the manufacture of bronze required considerable skill, and there is evidence that the Old Phoenicians on the coast had the monopoly over this process. They inhabited the coastal strip of the Levant, including that part of it later known as Philistia, although in the Middle Bronze Age, the Philistines had not yet arrived, and according to curses on them found in Egypt, it was still inhabited by the Anakim who were giants of men, also cursed by the Egyptians.

The story about the smiths in the first *Book of Samuel*, in Middle Bronze Age context (which it fits well), would read like this:

Now there was no smith to be found throughout all the land of the Hebrews, for the Kenites said: 'Lest the Hebrews make themselves swords or spears.' But every one of the Hebrews went down to the Kenites on the coast, to sharpen his ploughshare, his mattock, his axe or his sickle. And the charge was a pim for the ploughshares and for the mattocks, and a third of a shekel for sharpening the axes and for setting the goads. So on the day of the battle there was neither sword nor spear found in the hand of any of the people with Saul and Jonathan: but Saul and Jonathan his son had them.

David both conquered and formed a marriage alliance with the inhabitants of the coastal strip and with the Kenites. He also rallied troops from his possessions on the Nile, and it is specifically in Egypt that Solomon's chariots were made, where the guilds of smiths date back to Imhotep at least.

The second story seems to concern the very beginnings of chariot warfare, and is set on the Upper Euphrates where horse-drawn chariots were introduced to the Near East by the Mitanni.

David also defeated Hadadezer King of Zobah, toward Hamath, as he went to set up his monument at the river Euphrates. And David took from him a thousand chariots, seven thousand horsemen, and twenty thousand foot soldiers; and David hamstrung all the chariot horses, but left enough for a hundred chariots. And when the Syrians of Damascus came to help Hadadezer King of Zobah, David slew twenty-two thousand men of the Syrians. Then David put garrisons in Syria of Damascus; . . . And from Tibhath and from Cun, cities of Hadadezer, David took very much bronze; with it Solomon made the bronze sea and the pillars and the vessels of bronze.[6]

Whether Zobah can be identified with the territory of Subartu (the territory of the Mitanni) or not, the campaign was most definitely in that direction. David hamstrung the horses. As John Bright puts it, 'Amazing as it seems, David could find no use for this equipment; keeping only enough horses to draw a hundred chariots.' But it would make better sense at the very beginning of chariot warfare, just when it was introduced into the Ancient Near East.

The Bow

The second source of power for the West Semites was the new Asiatic or compound bow. The bow and arrow had been used before, but it was a feeble affair that played no decisive role in earlier battles. But the new bow that was introduced at this time was a formidable weapon, still a longbow but made of horn on the inside, wood in the middle, and gut and sinew on the outside. In order to draw the bow, the horn panels on the inside had to be compressed and the gut on the outside stretched as well as bending the wood. Such a weapon was a veritable gift of the gods for those who had it, and there are many stories about it, like those of the Bow of Aqhat in Canaanite myth, and the bow of Ulysses. I am inclined to think that the story of the bow which Jonathan gave to David was trivialized and derived from an older epic or legend first told in the Age of Myth when such bows were introduced.

When he had finished speaking to Saul, the soul of Jonathan was knit to the soul of David, and Jonathan loved him as his own soul ... Then Jonathan made a covenant with David, because he loved him as his own son. And Jonathan stripped himself of the robe that was upon him, and gave it to David, and his armour, and even his sword and his bow and his girdle. And David went out and was successful wherever Saul sent him; so that Saul set him over the men of war. And this was good in the sight of all the people . . . And the women sang to one another as they made merry.

'Saul has slain his thousands,
and David his ten thousands.'

Saul became insanely jealous and David was forced to go into hiding for fear of his life. Jonathan told Saul that David was in his home town to attend a yearly sacrifice for the new moon. Then Jonathan said to David:

Tomorrow is the new moon; and you will be missed, because your seat will be empty. And on the third day you will be greatly missed; then go to the place where you hid yourself when the matter was in hand, and remain beside yonder stone heap. And I will shoot three arrows to the side of it, as though I shot at a mark. And behold, I will send the lad, saying, 'Go, find the arrows.' If I say to the lad, 'Look, the arrows are on this side of you, take them,' then you are to come, for, as the Lord lives, it is safe for you and there is no danger. But if I say to the youth 'Look, the arrows are beyond you,' then go; for the Lord has sent you away . . .

In the morning Jonathan went out into the field to the appointment with David, and with him a little lad. And he said to his lad, 'Run and find the arrows which I shoot.' As the lad ran, he shot an arrow beyond him. And when the lad came to the place of the arrow which Jonathan had shot, Jonathan called after the lad and said, 'Is not the arrow beyond you?' . . . But the lad knew nothing; only Jonathan and David knew the matter. And Jonathan gave his weapons to his lad and said to him, 'Go and carry them to the city.' And as soon as the lad had gone, David rose from beside the stone heap and fell on his face to the ground, and bowed three times; and they kissed one another, and wept with one another, until David recovered himself.

> Then Jonathan said to David, 'Go in peace, foras-
> much as we have sworn both of us in the name of the
> Lord, saying, "The Lord shall be between me and you,
> and between my descendants and your descendants
> forever."' And he rose and departed; and Jonathan went
> into the city.[7]

Even without knowing similar legendary tales, this story
gives the impression that a heavenly bow was being bestowed, and that the alliance was between divine powers
and a king, rather than between friends.

Perhaps more relevant to the task in hand of relating the
Hebrew empire to the West Semite empire is the fact that
Saul was killed by an arrow. The battle pressed hard upon
Saul, and the archers found him; and he was badly wounded
by the archers . . . Therefore Saul took his own sword, and
fell upon it.[8]

This is the first time in the Hebrew chronicle that archery
plays a decisive role. As a result of it David decided that the
use of the bow must be taught to his Hebrew troops. And
archery plays an increasingly important part in warfare as
when Uriah and others were killed by the archers. Among
David's troops, the Benjaminites especially were organized
as the bowmen 'who could shoot arrows and sling stones
with either the right or the left hand'.

David laments for Saul and Jonathan:

> Thy glory, O Israel, is slain upon thy high places!
> How are the mighty fallen! . . .
> The bow of Jonathan turned not back . . .[9]

The time when the West Semite kings introduced this strong
compound bow into the area marks a turning point in the
descriptions of warfare. For the rest of the Bronze Age it
is clear from the correspondence of the time that a mere
handful of such bowmen were sufficient to defend a walled
city from an attacking army.

The Wealth

The archaeological record has not brought to light any special wealth for this period, but it is the Egyptian records that reveal the true picture. Nothing gets recycled so quickly and surely as wealth and it is the prodigious wealth of the New Empire in Egypt that most surely reveals the wealth of the Levant just before. The tomb of Tutankhamun is the best-known of the tombs found with much of its treasure intact, which are enough to give a vivid impression of the grandeur of that epoch – and also of the epoch just before.

The treasures of Egypt in the Bronze Age have, in their turn, long been plundered and recycled – perhaps some of its gold lies buried in Fort Knox now. But we know it was there, and we know where it came from.

Egyptian annals are explicit about what they took from Western Asia when they conquered and plundered it. First they drove the foreign rulers from their own land. And then they campaigned in the Levant, returning after each successful campaign with colossal booty. Hundreds of pounds of white gold, and hundreds of pounds of yellow gold. The empire of the West Semites in Asia was the chief source of the wealth of the new empire in Egypt, plundered by the first kings of Egypt to be called 'Pharaohs' (of the Great House).

Among the booty depicted on the walls of the Temple of Ammon in Karnak are the complete furnishings of a West Semite Temple which Velikovsky has shown match the furnishings of the Temple of Solomon, which are described in detail by the Hebrew chroniclers.

They also describe a little of his wealth:

> And the king made silver as common in Jerusalem as stone, and he made cedar as plentiful as the sycamore of the Shephelak.
> Moreover the fleet of Hiram which brought gold

from Ophir, brought from Ophir a very great amount the almug wood and precious stones. And the king made of the almug wood supports for the house of the Lord, and for the king's house, lyres also and harps for the singers; no such almug wood has come or been seen, to this day.

Now the weight of gold that came to Solomon in one year was six hundred and sixty-six talents of gold (each talent weighing 75–80 lbs), besides that which came from the traders and from the traffic of the merchants and from all the kings of Arabia and from the governors of the land.

The king also made a great ivory throne, and overlaid it with the finest gold . . . The like of it was never made in any kingdom. All King Solomon's drinking vessels were of pure gold, and all the vessels of the House of the Forest of Lebanon were of pure gold; none were of silver, it was not considered as anything in the days of Solomon.

For the king had a fleet of ships of Tarshish at sea with the fleet of Hiram. Once every three years the fleet of ships of Tarshish used to come bringing gold, silver, ivory, apes, and peacocks.

Thus King Solomon excelled all the kings of the earth in riches and in wisdom. And the whole earth sought the presence of Solomon to hear his wisdom, which God had put into his mind. Every one of them brought his present, articles of silver and gold, garments, myrrh, spices, horses, and mules, so much year by year.[10]

The Trade
Whatever the actual extent of the empire of the West Semites, there can be no doubt of their far-flung trading contacts. We have already mentioned the name of Khyan found at Knossos in Crete and at Baghdad in Persia.

The language of Crete, written as Linear A, has not been

deciphered fully, but if it is not wholly Semitic it is full of Semite 'loan' words, indicating close contacts with Western Asia. Leonard Woolley, in *A Forgotten Kingdom*, has traced the path of civilization from Mesopotamia across North Syria, via Alalakh which he excavated, to Crete.

Much is still obscure, but it seems that once the West Semite 'Habiru' empire is re-examined in the light thrown upon it by the biblical records of the Hebrew empire of David and Solomon, what has been obscure until now may become clear. For example, David's personal bodyguard was Cretan. And Solomon's fleet was away for three years at a stretch. Where did they go? Could this be the link between the so-called cyclopean masonry at Shechem and in Sardinia?

One thing is clear: the West Semites made the mistake of trading with all their neighbours in horses and chariots which had been the source of their power. And Solomon made the same mistake.

And Solomon's import of horses was from Egypt and Kue, and the king's traders received them from Kue at a price. A chariot could be imported from Egypt for six hundred shekels of silver, and a horse for a hundred and fifty; and so through the king's traders they were exported to all the kings of the Hittites and the kings of Syria.[11]

And in due course these kings returned in them armed for battle.

King Keret and King David

At first glance, the legend of King Keret bears no resemblance to the story of King David.

But the first important point is that, given the reconstruction proferred in this investigation, both kings lived at the same time, in the (late?) 17th century BC. Both kings were of legendary significance and founded a dynasty at the time when the so-called 'Hyksos' kings were consolidating Semite power in the Ancient Near East. In particular, the Levant was united by chains of fortress towns. The question is, how much room was there for *two* such legendary kings, both of whom founded a dynasty?

I have included below substantial portions of both texts which display the differences fully. And I have no intention of trying to dispose of these differences or to explain them away. But there are factors and circumstances to be borne in mind. The Keret legend from the library at Ugarit is a thousand years older than the version we have of David's biography. This may explain the differences in religion particularly – if there were reforms later as the Bible indicates. Furthermore the Keret legend would appear to be a version of the story used for cultic and ritual purposes, whereas the story of David seems to be derived from a ballad form once sung at banquets, as Professor Gordon suggests. Finally, there are only fragments of the Keret legend. If we had the whole story it might correspond more closely to the detailed biography of David's life.

With regard to the similarities:

a   The fragments we do have of the Keret legend seem to correspond most especially with the last three chapters of the story of David's life.

b   Both kings lived at a time when the horse and chariot were just being introduced into the Ancient Near East, facilitating the consolidation of power.

c   Texts from Crete of this period include, *Dawida is Chief*, and David had a bodyguard of Cretans, indicating how far-flung his power and trade contacts were.

d   Keret's titles include 'Servant of El', 'Gracious one of

El', 'The lad of El', 'The Generous One', and David is a favourite and servant of God, noted for his beauty, nobility and generosity.

e Keret ruled from the city of Heber, and David from Hebron.

f The reading is obscure, but Keret's massive armies may have included men of Asher and of Zebulon. David had 40,000 warriors from Asher and 50,000 from Zebulon who attended his coronation at Hebron.

g Keret's house had 'seven brothers yea eight sons of one mother'. Similarly, David is the eighth born.

h All Keret's sons died, and tidings reached David that 'all the king's sons are dead, not one is left.' But the rumour turned out to be false. However, David lost his child by Bathsheba, also his son, Amnon, and finally Absalom.

i Both kings mourned, then washed and rouged or anointed themselves, then ate.

j Keret obtained a new wife after a siege, possibly in Geshur, and they had a son, Yassib. One of David's wives was from Geshur and gave birth to Absalom.

k John Gray called Yassib the 'Canaanite (West Semite) Absalom' because they had much in common. Both tried to usurp the throne, claiming they would be better judges of the poor, the widow and the orphan.

l Keret's deathbed scene has parallels with that of King David; both are nursed by a female ministering angel.

m With regard to the succession, God announced to Keret that he would give the birthright to his youngest son. In David's case, Adonijah and others were passed over in favour of Solomon.

n Both kings and their offspring were blessed in similar fashion, as the new dynasty was established.

Of Keret: 'The sons of Keret were as the gods had promised, yea the daughters too. Asherat the goddess took note of his vow: if Keret breaks his vow then I vow to break his . . . A double blessing El gave Keret: highly exalted may he be among the congregation of the land. Keret will reach the sunset, even to the sundown will he reign.'

And of David: 'His seed shall endure forever. If his children break my statutes then I will visit their transgression with the rod . . .' 'Oh Lord with thy blessing let the house of thy servant be blessed forever.' 'I have made thee a great name' says the Lord, 'like unto the name of the great men that are in the earth.' And: 'His throne shall be established forever, as the sun before me.'

However, it is not, for me, the details themselves that are so significant, but the fact that they were recorded at all in both cases. We have very little biographical detail from the Bronze Age. In the last 2,500 years, biography and autobiography have been common enough, but this was not so in earlier times. So it is not so much the fact that both David and Keret mourned, ate, and then rouged themselves which is remarkable, but the fact it was recorded in both cases. From the fragments we have it is not improbable that the complete Keret text contained more biographical detail than any other single text from the Bronze Age. And likewise the account of David's reign is by far the most detailed biography in the whole of the Bible.

The Legend of King Keret[12]

Pertaining to 'Keret' . ∴.

> . . . The house of a king is destroyed,
> Who had seven brethren,
>> Eight mother's sons.
> Keret in offspring is ruined,
>> Keret is undermined of establishment.

His lawful wife he did find,
    His legitimate spouse.
He married the woman, and she 'departed'.
    He sees his offspring ruined,
    Wholly undermined his seat,
And in its entirety a posterity perishing,
    And in its totality a succession.
So he enters his cubicle and weeps,
    An inner chamber and cries.
His tears do drop
    Like shekels to the ground.
His bed is soaked by his weeping,
    And he falls asleep as he cries.
Sleep prevails over him, and he lies;
    Slumber, and he reclines.
And in his dream El descends,
    In his vision the Father of Man.
And he approaches asking Keret:
'What ails Keret that he weeps,
    The Beloved, Lad of El, that he cries?
Is it a kingship like Bull his father's he desires,
    Or authority like the Father of Man's?'
Grant I may beget children;
    Grant that I multiply 'kinsmen'. –
And Bull, his father El, replied:
'Enough for thee of weeping, Keret;
    Of crying, Beloved, Lad of El.
Do thou wash and rouge thee.
Take a lamb in thy hand,
    A lamb of sacrifice in thy right hand;
A kid in the grasp of thy hand,
    All thy most tempting food.
Take a turtle dove,
    Bird of sacrifice.
In a bowl of silver pour wine,
    Honey in a bowl of gold.
Go up to the top of a tower.

Bestride the top of the wall;
Lift up thy hands to heaven,
   Sacrifice to Bull, thy father El;
Honour Baal with thy sacrifice,
   Dagon's Son with thine oblation.
Then descend, Keret, from the housetops.
Prepare thou corn from the granaries,
   Wheat from the storehouses.
Let bread be baked for a fifth,
   Food for a sixth month.
Muster the people and let it come forth,
   The host of the troops of the people.
Yea, let come forth the assembled multitude,
   Thy troops, a mighty force:
Three hundred myriads;
Like the locusts that dwell on the steppe,
   Like grasshoppers on the borders of the desert. –
March a day and a second;
   A third, a fourth day;
   A fifth, a sixth day –
Lo! at the sun on the seventh:
   Thou arrivest at Udum the Great,
   Even at Udum the Grand.
– Now do thou attack the villages,
   Harass the towns.
Thine arrows shoot not into the city,
   Nor thy hand-stones flung headlong.
And behold, at the sun on the seventh,
   King Pabel will sleep
Till the sound of the neighing of his stallion,
   Till the sound of the braying of his he-ass,
Until the lowing of the plough ox,
   Until the howling of the watchdog.
Then will he send two messengers unto thee,
   Unto Keret, to the camp:
'Message of King Pabel: –
Take silver and yellow-glittering gold;

Friendship by covenant and vassalage for ever;
Take it, Keret,
  In peace, in peace.
  Withdraw, O Keret, from my court.
Vex not Udum the Great.'
Then send thou the two messengers back to him: –
'What need have I of silver and yellow-glittering gold;
  Friendship by covenant and vassalage
  for ever;
Nay, what's not in my house shalt thou give!
  Give me Lady Hurriya,
  The fair, thy first-begotten;
Whose fairness is like Anath's fairness,
  Whose beauty like Ashtoreth's beauty;
Whose eyeballs are the pureness of lapis,
  Whose pupils the gleam of jet;
  . . . Let me bask in the brightness of her eyes;
Whom in my dream El bestowed,
  In my vision the Father of Man.
And let her bear offspring to Keret,
  And a lad to the Servant of El.' –
Keret awoke, and lo, it was a dream;
Then washed he and roug'd him:
He went up to the top of a tower,
  Bestrode the top of a wall;
Lifted up his hands to heaven,
  Sacrificed to Bull, his Father El;
Honoured Baal with his sacrifice,
  Dagon's Son with his oblation.
Keret descended from the housetops.
He prepared corn from the granaries,
  Wheat from the storehouses.
He mustered the people
And forth came the assembled multitude,
  His troops, a mighty force:
Three hundred myriads.
They march a day and a second;

Then, at the sun on the third,
They come to the shrine of Asherah of Tyre,
Even that of Elath of Sidon.
There Keret the Noble vows:
'As Asherah of Tyre exists,
   As Elath of Sidon!
If Hurriya to my house I take,
   Bring the lass into my court,
Her double I'll give in silver,
   And her treble in gold.'

(And Keret besieged the town of Udum, and after some missing and damaged lines King Pabel consents to the marriage and sends his daughter who, he claims, is the embodiment of virtue and will be sorely missed by him and his people. He tells Keret that the people of Udum will wail, and follow her lamenting to the camp, as the cow moans for the calf, as the young of the herd moan for their mother. Keret fulfilled his vow to the goddesses of Tyre and Sidon, and when the wedding preparations have been made:)

Then came the companies of the gods.
   And Puissant Baal spake up:
'Now come, O Kindly One El Benign!
Wilt thou not bless Keret the Noble,
   Not beatify the Beloved, Lad of El?' –
A cup El takes in his hand,
   A flagon in his right hand.
El blesses Keret,
   Beatifies the Beloved, Lad of El:
'The woman thou tak'st, O Keret,
Shall bear seven sons unto thee;
   Yea, eight she'll produce for thee.
She shall bear Yassib the Lad,
   Who shall draw the milk of Asherah,
Suck the breasts of the maiden Anath,
   The two wet nurses of the gods.
Also, she shall conceive and bear daughters to thee.

To the youngest of them will I give the birthright.' –
The gods bless and proceed.
    The gods proceed to their tents,
    The family of El to their habitations.
And she conceives and bears son(s) to him,
    And conceives and bears daughters to him.
Lo! in seven years,
    The sons of Keret are even as was
    stipulated in the vows;
    The daughters, also, of Hurriya are even so.
And Asherah remembers his vows,
    Even Elath his dedications,
    And lifts up her voice and cries:
'Look, now. Doth Keret, then, break,
    Or alter vows?
So shall I break . . .' (Missing lines.)
His feet upon the footstool he sets.
    Loudly unto his wife he doth cry:
'Hearken, O Lady Hurriya!
Prepare the fattest of thy stall-fed ones;
    Open a jar of wine,
Summon my seventy peers,
    My eighty barons:
The peers of Khubur the Great,
    Khubur the Grand.'
    (10–13 lines broken and unintelligible.)
Lady Hurriya obeys.
Into her presence she causes his peers to come,
    Into her presence his barons she causes to come:
Into the house of Keret they come,
Hand to the bowl she stretches forth,
    Knife to the flesh she doth apply.
And Lady Hurriya declared:
'To eat, to drink have I summoned you:
    Your lord Keret hath a sacrifice.'
'At the setting of the sun Keret will come,
    As the sun goes down our lord;'

Into Keret's presence they enter.
    Like the speech of the peers is their speech.
In a vision . . . . . . Keret.

(*Translator's note*: The point of these banquets remains obscure owing to gaps in the text. Some 40 lines are missing, and there is some indication that Keret became ill. The passing years that elapse between the seventh year of Keret's marriage above, and the maturity of certain of their offspring, Elhau, Thitmanet as well as Yassib is likely to have been indicated in this lacuna.)

'Like a dog thine aspect is changed, like a cur thy
    joyous countenance.
Wilt thou die, then, father, like the mortals,
    Or thy joy change to mourning,
    To a woman's dirge, O father, my song?
For thee, father, weeps the mount of Baal,
    Zaphon, the sacred circuit.
The mighty circuit laments,
    The circuit broad of span:'
Into the presence of his father he goes,
    Weeping bitter tears,
    Giving forth his voice in weeping:
'Wilt thou die then, father, like the mortals,
How can it be said, "A son of El is Keret,
    An offspring of the Kindly One, and a holy being"?
Shall, then, a god die,
    An offspring of the Kindly One not live?'
And Keret the Noble answers:
'My son, weep not for me,
    Do thou not wail for me.
Call thy sister Thitmanet,
    A maid whose passion is strong.
    Let her weep and wail for me.
Straightway the youth Elhau
    His lance in his hand doth take,
His spear in his right hand,

And setteth out on a run.
Even as he arrives, it grows dark:
   His sister kindles a lamp.
As soon as she sees her brother,
   Her loins to the ground do break;
   Upon her brother's neck she weeps:
'Is thy sire Keret ill?'
The ploughmen raise their heads,
   Upward the growers of corn.
Spent is the bread corn from their jars,
   Spent the wine from their skin-bottles,
   Spent the oil from their jugs.

(As in the Grail legend famine appears to be linked with the
sickness of the king.)

And the Kindly One, El Benign, spake:
'Hearken, O carpenter-god Ilish –
   Ilish, carpenter of the house of Baal –
   And thy wives the carpenter-goddesses.
Go up upon the top of the structure,
   Upon the platform . . .
(Three lines defective and unintelligible,
   25 more missing.)
(Seven times, El the Benign asks:)
'Who among the gods can remove the illness,
   Driving out the malady?'
None among the gods answers him.
Then spake the Kindly One, El Benign:
'Sit ye, my sons, upon your seats,
   Upon your thrones of princeship.
I will work magic
   And will surely compass
The removal of illness,
   Driving out the malady.'
– With clay his hand he fills,
With goodly clay his fingers.

He . . . (moulded a female, named Sha'taqat,
   out of clay?)
   ' . . .
Death, do thou be broken;
Sha'taqat, do thou prevail.' –
(So Sha'taqat departs, over towns and villages she flies, to
the invalid, to the suffering one, and she proceeds to wash
the sweat from his brow.)
   His desire for bread she opens,
      His appetite for food.
   Death, on the one hand, is broken;
      Sha'taqat, on the other, has prevailed. –
   Then Keret the Noble commands,
      Raising his voice and crying
   'Hearken, O Lady Hurriya.
   Prepare a lamb that I may eat,
      A yeanling that I may dine.'
   Lady Hurriya hearkens.
   She prepares a lamb and he eats,
      A yeanling and he dines.
   Behold a day and a second,
      Keret returns to his former estate;
   He sits upon the throne of kingship;
      Upon the dais, the seat of authority.
   Now, Yassib sits in the palace,
      And his inward parts do instruct him:
   'Go unto thy father, Yassib;
      Go unto thy father and speak,
      Repeat unto Keret the Noble:
   "List and incline thine ear.
   (one couplet unintelligible)
   Thou hast let thy hand fall into mischief."
   Thou judgest not the cause of the widow,
      Nor adjudicat'st the case of the wretched.
   Having become a brother of the sickbed,
   A companion of the bed of the suffering,
Descend from the kingship – I'll reign;

> From thine authority – I'll sit enthroned."' –
> Yassib the Lad departs,
> > Enters his father's presence,
> > And lifts up his voice and cries:
> 'Hearken, I pray thee, Keret the Noble!
> > List and incline thine ear.
> (here again the unintelligible couplet)
> Thou hast let thy hand fall into mischief.
> Thou judgest not the cause of the widow,
> > Nor adjudicat'st the case of the wretched;
> > Driv'st not out them that prey on the poor;
> Feed'st not the fatherless before thee,
> > The widow behind thy back,
> Having become a brother of the sickbed,
> > A companion of the bed of suffering,
> Descend from the kingship – I'll reign;
> > From thine authority – I'll sit enthroned.' –
> And Keret the Noble makes answer:
> 'May Horon break, O my son,
> > May Horon break thy head,
> > Ashtoreth name of Baal thy pate.
> May'st thou fall into . . .'
> (last line unintelligible)

Written by Elimelech. Donated by Niqmadd, King of Ugarit.

The Ballad of King David[13]

Now David was the son of an Ephraithite of Bethlehem in Judah, named Jesse, who had eight sons . . . David was the youngest; . . .

So all the elders of Israel come to the king at Hebron; and King David made a covenant with them at Hebron before the Lord, and they anointed David king over Israel.

David took the stronghold of Zion, that is, the city of

David. And David said on that day, 'Whoever would attack the Jabusites, let him get up the watershaft to attack the lame and the blind, who are hated by David's soul.' Therefore it is said, 'The blind and the lame shall not come into the house.' And David dwelt in the stronghold, and called it the city of David.

And Hiram King of Tyre sent messengers to David, and cedar trees, also carpenters and masons who built David a house. And David perceived that the Lord established him king over Israel, and that he had exalted his kingdom for the sake of his people Israel.

And David took more concubines and wives from Jerusalem, after he came from Hebron; and more sons and daughters were born to David . . .

The word of the Lord came to Nathan, 'Go and tell my servant David, . . . I will make for you a great name, like the name of the great ones of the earth . . . I will raise up your offspring after you, who shall come forth from your body, and I will establish his kingdom . . . I will be his father, and he shall be my son. When he commits iniquity, I will chasten him with the rod of men, . . . but I will not take my steadfast love from him . . .' In accordance with all these words, and in accordance with this vision, Nathan spoke to David. Then King David went in and sat before the Lord, and said, 'Oh Lord God, thou hast spoken also of thy servant's house for a great while to come, and hast shown me future generations . . . Thou hast promised this good thing to thy servant.'. . . .

Articles of silver, of gold, and of bronze, . . . King David dedicated to the Lord, together with the silver and gold which he dedicated from all the nations he subdued.

In the spring of the year, the time when kings go forth to battle, . . . it happened, late one afternoon, when David arose from his couch and was walking upon the roof of the king's house, that he saw from the roof a woman bathing; and the woman was very beautiful. And David sent and inquired about the woman. And one said, 'Is not this

Bathsheba, the daughter of Eliam, the wife of Uriah the Hittite?' So David sent messengers, and took her; and she came to him, and he lay with her . . . Then she returned to her house. And the woman conceived. And she sent and told David, 'I am with child.'

. . . In the morning David wrote a letter to (his commander) Joab, and sent it by the hand of Uriah. In the letter he wrote, 'Set Uriah in the forefront of the hardest fighting, and then draw back from him, that he may be struck down, and die.' And as Joab was besieging the city . . . some of the servants of David among the people fell. Uriah the Hittite was slain also. Then Joab sent and told David all the news about the fighting . . . 'Your servant Uriah the Hittite is dead also.'

When the wife of Uriah heard that Uriah her husband was dead, she made lamentation for her husband. And when the mourning was over, David sent and brought her to his house, and she became his wife, and bore him a son. But the thing that David had done displeased the Lord.

And the Lord sent Nathan to David. He came to him and said to him '. . . Because by this deed you have utterly scorned the Lord, the child that is born to you shall die.' Then Nathan went to his house.

And the Lord struck the child that Uriah's wife bore to David, and it became sick. David therefore besought God for the child; and David fasted, and went in and lay all night upon the ground. On the seventh day the child died. And the servants of David feared to tell him . . . but when David saw that his servants were whispering together David perceived that the child was dead; and David said to his servants, 'Is the child dead?' They said, 'He is dead.' Then David arose from the earth, and washed and anointed himself, and changed his clothes; and he went into the house of the Lord, and worshipped; he then went to his own house; and when he asked, they set food before him, and he ate. He said, 'While the child was still alive, I fasted and wept. . . But now he is dead; why should I fast? Can

I bring him back again? I shall go to him, but he will not return to me.'

Then David comforted his wife Bathsheba and went in to her, and lay with her; and she bore a son, and he called his name Solomon. And the Lord loved him, and sent a message by Nathan the prophet; so he called his name Jedidiah (the beloved of the Lord).

Now Joab fought against Rabbah, of the Ammonites, and took the royal city. And Joab sent messengers to David, and said, 'I have fought against Rabbah; moreover, I have taken the city of waters. Now, then, gather the rest of the people together, and encamp against the city, and take it; lest I take the city, and it be called by my name.'

... Now Absalom, David's son, had a beautiful sister, whose name was Tamar; and after a time Amnon, David's son, loved her ... So Amnon lay down, and pretended to be ill. So Tamar went to her brother's house, where he was lying down ... Then Amnon said to Tamar, 'Bring the food into my chamber, that I may eat from your hand.' But when she brought them near him to eat, he took hold of her, and said to her 'Come lie with me, my sister.' She answered him, 'No.' But he would not listen to her; and being stronger than she, he forced her, and lay with her ...

Absalom hated Amnon, because he had forced his sister Tamar. After two full years, Absalom ... invited all the king's sons ... Then Absalom commanded his servants, 'Mark when Amnon's heart is merry with wine, and when I say to you, "Strike Amnon," then kill him.'

While they were on the way, tidings came to David, 'Absalom has slain all the king's sons, and not one of them is left.' Then the king arose, and rent his garments, and lay on the earth, and all his servants who were standing by, rent their garments, and lay on the earth ... David's brother said, 'Let not my lord suppose that they have killed all the young men the king's sons for Amnon alone is dead, for by the command of Absalom this has been determined from the day he forced his sister Tamar.'

So Absalom fled, and went to Geshur, and was there three years ... Then the king said to Joab, 'Go, bring back the young man Absalom ... Let him dwell apart in his own house; he is not to come into my presence.'

Absalom got himself a chariot and horses, and fifty men to run before him. And Absalom used to rise early and stand beside the way of the gate; and when any man had a suit to come before the king for judgement, Absalom would call him, and say, 'See, your claims are good and right; but there is no man deputed by the king to hear you ... Oh that I were judge in the land! Then every man with a suit or cause might come to me, and I would give him justice.' ... so Absalom stole the hearts of the men of Israel.

And at the end of four years, Absalom ... arose and went to Hebron, but Absalom sent secret messengers throughout all the tribes of Israel saying, 'As soon as you hear the sound of the trumpet, then say, "Absalom is king at Hebron!"' ... And the conspiracy grew strong, and the people with Absalom kept increasing.

Then David mustered the men who were with him, and set over them commanders of thousands and commanders of hundreds. And David sent forth the army ... So the army went out into the field against Israel; and the battle was fought in the forest of Ephraim. And the men of Israel were defeated there by the servants of David and the slaughter there was very great on that day, twenty thousand men.

Absalom was riding upon his mule, and the mule went under the thick branches of a great oak, and his head caught fast in the oak, and he was left hanging between heaven and earth, while the mule that was under him went on. Joab ... took three darts in his hand, and thrust them into the heart of Absalom, while he was still alive in the oak ... And they took Absalom, and threw him into a great pit in the forest, and raised over him a very great heap of stones; and all Israel fled every one to his own home. Now Absalom in his lifetime had taken and set up for himself the pillar which is in the

King's Valley, for he said 'I have no son to keep my name in remembrance,' . . .

And the king was deeply moved, and went up to the chamber over the gate, and wept; and as he went, he said, 'O my son Absalom, my son, my son Absalom! Would I had died instead of you, O Absalom, my son, my son.'

. . . Now there was a famine in the days of David for three years, year after year. And David sought the face of the Lord. And the Lord said, 'There is bloodguilt on Saul and on his house, because he put the Gibeonites to death.'

. . . The king took the two sons of Rizpah, the daughter of Aiah, whom she bore to Saul, and the five sons of Merab the daughter of Saul, and he gave them into the hands of the Gibeonites, and they hanged them on the mountain before the Lord, and the seven of them perished together.

Then Rizpah the daughter of Aiah took sackcloth, and spread it for herself on the rock, from the beginning of harvest until rain fell upon them from the heavens; and she did not allow the birds of the air to come upon them by day, or the beasts of the field by night. David went and took the bones of Saul and the bones of his son Jonathan . . . and they gathered the bones of those who were hanged. And they buried the bones of Saul and his son Jonathan . . . After that God heeded supplications for the land . . .

Now King David was old and advanced in years; and although they covered him with clothes, he could not get warm. Therefore his servants said to him, 'Let a young maiden be sought for my lord the king, and let her wait upon the king, and be his nurse; let her lie in your bosom that my lord the king may be warm.' So they sought for a beautiful maiden throughout all the territory of Israel, and found Abishag the Shunammite, and brought her to the king. The maiden was very beautiful . . .

So Bathsheba went to the king into his chamber. Now the king was very old, and Abishag the Shunammite was ministering to him, she said to him, '. . . The eyes of all

Israel are upon you, to tell them who shall sit upon the throne of my lord the king after him ...' And the king swore, saying, 'As the Lord lives, who has redeemed my soul out of every adversity, as I swore to you by the Lord, the God of Israel, saying, "Solomon your son shall reign after me, and he shall sit upon my throne in my stead"; even so will I do this day.' ...

Then David slept with his fathers, and was buried in the city of David. And the time that David reigned over Israel was forty years; he reigned seventy years in Hebron, and thirty-three years in Jerusalem. So Solomon sat upon the throne of David his father; and his kingdom was firmly established.

> His line shall endure forever,
> His throne as long as the sun before me.
> Like the moon it shall be established forever;
> It shall stand firm while the skies endure.
> I will establish his line for ever,
> And his throne as the days of the heavens.
> If his children forsake my law
> And do not walk according to my ordinances,
> If they violate my statutes
> And do not keep my commandments,
> Then I will punish their transgression with the
> rod ...

The Temples in Avaris, Kadesh and Jerusalem

By the time the chroniclers were writing in the seventh century BC there was only one temple for the Hebrew-speaking people. It was unique. But it was unique because it was the last remaining temple of its type, the sole survivor. In the seventeenth century BC there were many other temples of the same type and structure, for the ancestors of those Hebrew-speaking people to worship in. Their foundations

117

have been excavated by archaeologists, and they are mentioned in Egyptian records. Even the Hebrew chroniclers seem to mention inadvertently other houses at such places as Shechem, Shiloh and Bethel. For the moment, it is enough to point out that there was only one temple standing at the time when the chroniclers were writing, and any story about a temple might easily enough be associated with this temple.

Everything about the temple in Jerusalem suggests that, like the first ramparts around the city, it was a survivor from the Late Bronze Age, when megalithic structures of that type were common. First, we shall look at the Egyptian text about the magnificent temple built in the West-Semite capital at Avaris during their period of rule in Lower Egypt:

> And it happened that King Sekenenre was Ruler of the Southern City (Thebes) ... while the chieftain Apophis was in Avaris and the entire land paid tribute to him in full, as well as with all good things of Egypt. Then King Apophis took Sutekh (Saphon) to himself as lord, and served not any God which was in the entire land except Sutekh. And he built a temple of fair and everlasting work by the side of the house of King Apophis, and he arose every day to make the daily sacrifice to Sutekh, and the officials of His Majesty bore garlands of flowers exactly as is done in the temple of Pre-Harakte.[14]

Because the West Semites first moved their capital to Avaris before they fell back on Jerusalem, this could be an Egyptian account of the house of the Lord beside the house of the king, which took Solomon twenty years to build.

Another such temple is the subject of an epic poem unearthed at Ugarit. Its context is the period when the West Semites were at the height of their power, and had legendary wealth. But in many details it matches the

118

descriptions of Solomon's temple. But first the relevant parts of the epic poem:

> Let a house be built for (the Lord, the Rider
> of the Clouds),
> A house of cedar, yea a house of brick.
> The mountains shall bring thee much silver,
> The hills a treasure of gold;
> So build thou a silver and gold house.
> Quickly, raise up a palace,
> In the midst of the fastness of Zaphon.
> A thousand fields, the house shall cover,
> A myriad of acres the palace.
> Quoth Kothar: 'A window I will make in the house,
> A casement within the palace . . .
> As for (the Lord) his house is built,
> From Lebanon and its trees, his palace is raised.
> The (Powerful Lord) exults.
> He slaughters both neat and small cattle,
> Rams and one-year-old calves, lambs and kids
> He sates the gods with jars of wine,
> So eat the gods and drink.
> They sate them with fatness abundant
> While drinking the wine from flagons;
> From gold cups the blood of vines.'[15]

Unlike the detailed biography of David, the Hebrew account of the reign of Solomon is comparatively short and largely taken up with the building of a temple:

> And so I propose to build a house for the name of the Lord my God . . . Now therefore command that cedars of Lebanon be cut for me; . . .
> And Hiram sent to Solomon, saying, '. . . I am ready to do all you desire in the matter of cedar and cypress timber. My servants shall bring it down to the sea from

Lebanon; and I will make it into rafts to go by sea to the place you direct, . . .'

And Solomon overlaid the inside of the house with pure gold, and he drew chains of gold across, in front of the inner sanctuary, and overlaid it with gold. And he overlaid the whole house with gold, until all the house was finished . . . The floor of the house he overlaid with gold in the inner and outer rooms . . . And in the eleventh year, in the month of Bul, which is the eighth month, the house was finished in all its parts, and according to all its specifications. He was seven years in building it.

And King Solomon and all the congregation of Israel, who had assembled before him, were with him before the ark, sacrificing so many sheep and oxen that they could not be counted or numbered . . .

Then Solomon said,
'The Lord has set the sun in the heavens,
But has said that he would dwell in thick darkness.
I have built thee an exalted house,
A palace for thee to dwell in for ever.'

Solomon offered as peace offerings to the Lord twenty-two thousand oxen and twenty thousand sheep . . . So Solomon held the feast at that time, and all Israel with him, a great assembly, from the entrance of Hamath to the Brook (River?) of Egypt, before the Lord our God seven days.[16]

In both the West Semite and the Hebrew accounts there are descriptions of the furnishings and vessels in the temples.

From the library of Ugarit:

(The Deft One) Hayyin, would go up to the bellows,
In the hands of the Craftsman God, Kothar, would be the tongs,

To melt silver, to beat out gold.
He'd melt silver by the thousands (of shekels),
Gold he'd melt by the myriads,
For a gorgeous dais cast in silver,
Coated with a film of gold,
A gorgeous throne resting above a gorgeous
Footstool,
A gorgeous couch, overspread with gold.
A gorgeous table which is filled with all manner of
vessels,
Made from the ore of the earth,
Gorgeous bowls shaped like small beasts
Pillars sculptured with wild beasts.[17]

And from the description of Solomon's temple:

The king also made a great ivory throne and overlaid it
with the finest gold. The throne had six steps, and at
the back of the throne was a calf's head, and on each
side of the seat were arm rests and two lions standing
beside the arm rests, while twelve lions stood there,
one on each end of a step on the six steps. The like of
it was never made in any kingdom. All King Solomon's
drinking vessels were of gold, . . .[18]
So Solomon made all the vessels that were in the
house of the Lord: the golden altar, the golden table for
the bread of the Presence, the lampstands of pure gold,
. . . the flowers, the lamps, and the tongs, of gold; the
cups, snuffers, basins, dishes for incense and firepans
of pure gold; . . .
   He cast two pillars of bronze . . . Then he made the
molten sea . . . It stood upon twelve oxen . . . He also
made the ten stands of bronze: they had panels and
the panels were set in the frames and on the panels that
were set in the frames were lions, oxen and cherubim.[19]

Velikovsky has shown that all these vessels, item for item,

121

formed part of the plunder taken from West Semite city of Kadesh by Tuthmosis III, who had them inscribed piece by piece, item by item on the walls of the great Egyptian temple at Thebes where they have remained to this day. Only the names are changed – old Thebes is modern Luxor.

The Hebrew chroniclers appear to have preserved a record of this same event:

> In the fifth year of king Rehoboam (son of Solomon) because they had been unfaithful to the Lord, Shishak king of Egypt came up against Jerusalem with twelve hundred chariots and sixty thousand horsemen. And the people were without number who came with him from Egypt – Libyans, Sukki-im, and Ethiopians. And he took the fortified cities of Judah, and came as far as Jerusalem . . . he took away the treasures of the house of the Lord, and the treasures of the king's house; he took away everything. He also took away the shields of gold which Solomon had made.[20]

The Question of Hammurabi and the Legacy of the Akkadian Language

In the seventeenth and sixteenth centuries BC, at the time when Egypt was governed by the West Semite Habiru, Mesopotamia was also ruled by the West Semites. At more or less the same time as the West Semites were driven out of Egypt, their dynastic power in Babylon was also terminated. The question is, could Egypt and Mesopotamia have been the two extreme ends of a single West Semite empire at the time, with garrisons and fortress towns along the great King's Highway between the two?

It has to be admitted that there is not much evidence either for or against this. But putting together the shreds of evidence, there seems to me more for it than against.

The Hebrew chroniclers themselves made no such claims,

but by the time they were writing, the New Assyrians and the New Babylonians were their deadly enemies. In their time it was the ruthless armies of New Assyria that crushed Israel, and New Babylon destroyed Jerusalem soon after, and deported the inhabitants. It is hardly any wonder if they disclaim friendship with such neighbours. Nevertheless, between the lines of their text there are signs that these Eastern neighbours were once part of a unified Semite confederacy, and comprised the tribal states of Agade and Asshur (Gad and Asher). Isaiah speaks of the High Road between Assyria and Egypt and the traffic of people between the two, which was made a very real possibility by the light two-wheeled chariots drawn by two horses, with garrisons for changing the horses all the way along the 1,000 mile long route.

The great founder and ruler of the First Babylon was Hammurabi who was one of the great figures of the Bronze Age. His name, or title, 'Hammurabi', means 'Father of the West Semites'. Parts of his great law code have been included verbatim in the Bible. He himself is known to have compiled an early book comparable with the Hebrew Bible entitled the *Hammurabi Bible*, and when his Babylon fell, it was lamented for many centuries throughout the Semite world.

The Hebrew chroniclers were no exception: they also preserved a record of this disaster. The oracle against Babylon, in the context of the Bronze Age, which is the only context it fits, would read like this:

Behold I am stirring up the Mitanni and
    Hittites against them,
(those peoples later called the Medes)
who have no regard for silver
and do not delight in gold.
Their bows will slaughter the young men;
they will have no mercy on the fruit of the womb;
their eyes will not pity children.

And Babylon, the glory of kingdoms,
the splendour and pride of the Chaldeans
will be like Sodom and Gomorrah
when God overthrew them.
It will never be inhabited
or dwelt in for all generations;
no Arab will pitch his tent there,
no shepherds will make their flocks lie down there.
But the wild beasts will lie down there,
and its houses will be full of howling creatures;
there ostriches will dwell,
and there satyrs will dance.
Hyenas will cry in its towers,
and jackals in the pleasant palaces;
its time is close at hand
and its days will not be prolonged.[21]

Many generations of scholars considered that Hammurabi, the founder of this 'glory of kingdoms' was ruler of a considerable empire, although how considerable was by no means clear from the evidence. Indeed it was so unclear that, on account of one letter which has recently come to light, the standard version of history has now reduced him to a petty princeling ruling only Babylon and its immediate surroundings. The letter is from a bombastic petty princeling who challenges the power of Hammurabi and, from this, it has been argued that Hammurabi was no more powerful than that petty princeling. But following the same argument one would be forced to conclude that Queen Victoria's empire was no more extensive than that of the Boers . . .

For me it doesn't feel right. I don't think petty princelings draw up influential law codes, and compile the earliest known version of a Bible. I don't think an insignificant figure would have been the founder of such a significant place as the first Babylon.

Having mulled over the shreds of evidence that there are, I have reached the conclusion that he was one of the West

Semite rulers who, according to the Egyptian chronicler Manetho, spent only the summer months in Egypt. I think he could have reached the other end of his empire in ten days in an emergency. But in the ordinary way I think he probably spent spring and autumn in his homeland, the Levant, en route between the two extremes of his empire, Egypt and Mesopotamia.

It has always been argued that he could not have had any territory in the Levant because he never campaigned there. But if he was a West Semite, as his name indicates, then he would have no need to campaign in his native land. There is no conclusive proof of this. Indeed, the evidence of any sort is very scanty, but for one overriding consideration.

It is well known and indeed obvious, that in order to run an empire it is essential to have one common language spoken throughout its territories. This language is often left as a legacy after the empire has collapsed and its territories carved up. This is how English has become the common language of India.

Similarly, Mesopotamian was the common language of the whole Ancient Near East from the time when the West empire, with its fortress towns along the route between Egypt and Assyria, collapsed. So, in the reign of Akhenaten we find everybody writing to each other in the Mesopotamian language. Indeed, we also find a unified world where an Assyrian could be issued with a diplomatic pass to travel through the Levant to visit Egypt.

But when was this unity achieved? How did it come about? And why the Mesopotamian language, Akkadian? Why did West Semites who spoke and wrote Hebrew, and the Egyptians whose writing was hieroglyphs, correspond with each other in a language which belonged to neither of them?

This piece of evidence becomes more significant the more you think about it. The New Empire of the Pharaohs never ruled in Mesopotamia, which was conquered by the Mitanni and Hittites. At the time of the New Empire, the

Near East was not a unity, but was carved up between Hittites, Mitanni and Pharaohs. There would have been no occasion to insist on a single unified language throughout, as the usual translators would have been sufficient.

Everything points to the previous epoch as the time when the powerful West Semite imperial monarchs could have imposed a common diplomatic language in order to run the affairs of their empire.

But still the question remains: why Akkadian? It makes no sense at all unless they were ruling Mesopotamia. And they were, or at least kings with West Semite names were ruling Mesopotamia. So it is just a question of working out the connection between these West Semite monarchs and those who ruled in Egypt.

If they were the same imperial monarchs, then there was every reason for choosing Akkadian as the imperial diplomatic language, because it was the common root language of their ancestors. It would be like choosing Latin as the common language for ruling an empire of people speaking the Romance languages – as was done.

The language of Abraham and of Sargon the Great was chosen as the second language of the whole empire of Hammurabi, Father of the West Semites.

The Fragmented Hebrew Empire

The battle of Megiddo marked the end of West Semite supremacy in the Near East and, after that, even their home territory became a vassal state of Egypt. It wasn't just vast quantities of plunder, like yellow gold, white gold and all the furnishings of a magnificent temple that Tuthmosis III took, but also many Hebrew slaves, some of them named in Egyptian lists. Their names have been identified by Professor Albright with familiar Hebrew names:

Samson	Dodavahu
Job	Menahem
Ahab	Saphira

There were hundreds of others numbered, but not named, who were taken back into Egypt as slaves. Some of them were important princes, and held high positions in the Egyptian administration for generations to come.

Not only the Egyptians, but the Hittites and the Mitanni make frequent mention of the Hebrews (Habiru) in this period. Many of them had become mercenaries or charioteers for the neighbouring powers. But they were found in every trade from the highest to the lowest slaves. Their names indicated their mixed nationality, they were feared as marauders, plunderers. All this accords well with a time when the Hebrew empire had been smashed and fragmented, the vast armies of the former princes had been broken up without pay, and were looking for employment or for plunder.

The Hebrew chroniclers appear to have found scattered allusions to this period in the ancient texts from which they were working and sometimes they worked the ancient fragments into a prophecy or a curse:

Then the Lord will bring on you and your offspring extraordinary afflictions, afflictions severe and lasting and sickness grievous and lasting. And he will bring upon you again all the diseases of Egypt, which you were afraid of; and they shall cleave to you ... Whereas you were as the stars of heaven for multitude, you shall be left few in number; because you did not obey the voice of the Lord your God. And as the Lord took delight in doing you good and multiplying you, so the Lord will take delight in bringing ruin upon you and destroying you, and you shall be plucked off the land which you are entering to take possession of it. And the Lord will scatter you among all peoples, from one end of the earth to the other; ... And among

these nations you shall find no ease, and there shall
be no rest for the sole of your foot; . . . your life shall
hang in doubt before you; night and day you shall be
in dread, and have no assurance of your life. In the
morning you shall say, 'Would it were evening!' And
at evening you shall say, 'Would it were morning!' . . .
And the Lord will bring you back in ships to Egypt, a
journey which I promised that you should never make
again; and there you shall offer yourselves for sale to
your enemies as male and female slaves, but no man
will buy you.[22]

For several generations, many of the Hebrew people were
slaves to the Pharaohs in the New Empire of Egypt. Some
of them may have worked on the colossal temple at Luxor
(which was big enough to house the Vatican or St Paul's
Cathedral) where Tuthmosis III's triumphant campaigns
against them are inscribed on the walls. Others later no
doubt were among the bondsmen who built Pithom and
Raamses.

Meanwhile, their homeland had remained a vassal state
of Egypt, and the Hebrew chroniclers have preserved a
fragment of tradition about this Egyptian occupation.

The word of the Lord came to (the prophet) Shemaiah:
'They have humbled themselves; 'I will not destroy
them but I will grant them some deliverance, and
my wrath shall not be poured out upon Jerusalem by
the hand of the Pharaoh. Nevertheless they shall be
servants to him, that they may know my service and
the service of the kingdoms of the countries.'[23]

And it is in the context of this prophecy that the Pharaoh
carried away the treasures of the Temple as part of his
booty.

Occupation breeds resistance, and it wasn't long before
the Habiru were joining forces as freedom-fighters to throw

off the yoke of the Pharaohs. This resistance to the occupation is remarkably well documented in a large number of
letters found in the ruins of Akhenaten's ancient capital.

The Pharaoh's vassal-lords in Western Asia complained of
the growing menace of the Hebrews. From these hundreds
of letters those of Abdi-hiba, regent of Jerusalem, give a
vivid picture:[24]

> To the king my lord,
> At the two feet of my lord, the king, seven times and
> seven times I fall down . . . They slander me to the king,
> the lord: 'Abdi-Hiba has become faithless to the king,
> his lord.' . . . Why should I practise mischief against
> the king, the lord? As long as the king, my lord, lives
> I will say . . . 'Why do you love the Habiru and hate
> the regents?' . . . The Habiru plunder all lands of the
> king. The land of the king, the lord, is devastated and
> many have deserted. If archers are here this year, then
> the lands of the king will remain; but if archers are not
> here then the lands of the king are lost.

And:

> Verily the king has set his name upon the land of
> Jerusalem forever. Therefore he cannot abandon the
> lands of Jerusalem . . . Behold, I am a shepherd of the
> king, and I am one who bears the tribute of the king
> . . . Twenty-one maidens and eighty prisoners I gave
> . . . Although a man sees the facts, yet the two eyes
> of the king, my lord, do not see; for hostility is firm
> against me . . . Now the Habiru are taking the cities
> of the king.
> No regent is left to the king, my lord; all are lost.

But the Hebrew princes were also regents of the Pharaoh
and denied any conspiracy, although it became clear they
were lying.

Abdi-Ashirta wrote:

> Behold, I am a servant of the king, a dog of his house,
> and the whole land of (the West Semites) I guard for
> the king, my lord . . .
>   Behold all the viceroys of the king seek selected
> troops to snatch the lands from my hand . . .
>   What lies did the regents tell thee? . . .
>   So let the king hear my words, for the enmity against
> me is mighty . . .
>   And the words the king, my lord, has spoken to me,
> I have truly heard; I will truly obey . . .

And from his Hebrew son, Azira:

> Even now I am not guilty: not the least thing have I
> done against the king. I am thy servant forever and my
> sons are thy servants.
>   O king, my lord, give me servants and chariots and
> I will protect the land for the king.
>   And all that the regents have given, that will I also
> verily give.

And from Aziki to Dudu, called the mouthpiece of all the
foreign lands at the court of Akhenaten:

> Whatever is the wish of my lord the king, let him write
> and I will perform it. Let him know the lands of the West
> Semites are his lands, and my house is his house.

But Rib-Addi, viceroy of Gubna, like the viceroy of
Jerusalem, was more loyal to the Pharaoh than the Hebrew
leaders Abdi-Ashirta and his son Azira. He wrote to his
friend at court:

> Why hast thou held back and not spoken to the king,
> thy lord, in order that thou mayest march forth with

the archers, and that thou mayest fall upon the land of the West Semites? If they perceive that the archers have gone forth, they will leave even their cities and depart. Dost thou not know of the land of the West Semites that it is an abode of mighty men ... Are they not friendly with Abdi-Ashirta? ... And so they await day and night for the departure of the archers and say: 'We would join with them' ... Abdi-Ashirta wrote to the people: 'Kill your lord', and they joined the Hebrew-plunderers, then said the regents: 'Thus will he do to us'. And so all the lands will join with the Hebrew-plunderers ... And if the king should then march forth, all lands would be hostile to him, and what could he do for us then? Thus have they formed a conspiracy with one another ... and like that birds lie in a net, so am I in Gubna.

It isn't difficult to see the parallels between this period and the Hebrew account of the fragmentation of Solomon's empire shortly after his death.

First, in the correspondence between Egypt and Asia, there are long letters concerned with the elaborate arrangements for a marriage alliance between the royal house of Mitanni and the Pharaohs. The Mitanni were the enemies of the West Semites, and one of their powerful Eastern neighbours. The Hebrew chronicle relates that the Lord raised up an adversary against Solomon who was married into the Pharaoh's house. In David's reign Hedad had fled to Egypt, in the hands of his father's servants, as he was still a child.

They set out from Midian, and ... came to Egypt, to Pharaoh king of Egypt, who gave him a house, and assigned him an allowance of food and gave him land. And Hadad found great favour in the sight of Pharaoh, so that he gave him in marriage the sister of his own wife, the sister of Tahpenes the queen ...

> Rezon the son of Eliada . . . was also an adversary of
> Israel all the days of Solomon . . . And he gathered men
> about him and became leader of a marauding band, . . .
> doing mischief.[25]

And towards the end of Solomon's reign:

> Ahijah (the prophet) had clad himself with a new gar-
> ment . . . and laid hold of the new garment that was
> on him, and tore it into twelve pieces. And he said to
> Jeroboam '. . . Behold I am about to tear the kingdom
> from the hand of Solomon . . . Yet to his son I will give
> one tribe.'[26]

After the death of Solomon, the succession was divided as
well as reduced, and all the treasures of the temple were
taken by the Pharaohs. The kings of Judah became the vas-
sals of Egypt. But the Hebrew kings (or viceroys?) Abijam
and his son Asa seem to have been involved in intrigues,
skirmishes and battles that recall those of Abdi-Ashirta and
his son Azira, who were rallying the Hebrews against the
foreign domination of Egypt.

> And (Asa) said to Judah, 'Let us build these cities, and
> surround them with walls and towers, gates and bars;
> the land is still ours, because we have sought the Lord
> our God . . .'
> So they built and prospered. And Asa had an army
> of three hundred thousand from Judah, armed with
> bucklers and spears, and two hundred and eighty
> thousand men from Benjamin that carried shields and
> drew bows; all these were mighty men of valour.
> In the words of Azariah speaking to Asa: 'For a long
> time Israel was without the true God, and without a
> teaching priest, and without law; . . . In those times
> there was no peace to him who went out or to him
> who came in, for great disturbances afflicted all the

inhabitants of the lands. They were broken in pieces, nation against nation and city against city, for God troubled them with every sort of distress. But you, take courage! Do not let your hands be weak, for your work shall be rewarded.' . . . When Asa heard these words . . . he took courage . . .

Then Asa took silver and gold from the treasures of the house of the Lord and the king's house, and sent them to Benhadad king of Syria, . . . saying, 'Let there be a league between me and you, as between my father and your father; behold I am sending to you silver and gold; go, break your league with Baasha . . .' And Benhadad hearkened to King Asa and sent the commanders of his armies against the cities of Israel, and they conquered Ijon, Dan, Abel-maim and all the store-cities of Naphtali.[27]

The Last Viceroys of the Pharaoh: Jehosaphat and Zimri

In *Ages in Chaos*, Velikovsky's study of ancient history up until the reign of King Akhenaten, he compares the names of Jehosaphat's commanders in the Hebrew chronicle with names that appear in the letters to Akhenaten from his viceroys in Western Asia. All scholars are agreed that the list of commanders is very old indeed.

The brief life of Zimri, a servant who slew his king in the city of Tirzah while the king was getting drunk in the house of another of the servants, seems to resemble the situation in the letters to Akhenaten where the servants, from the West Semite populace, were urged by the Habiru leaders to overthrow and kill the regents and then oust the occupation forces. Just as Zimri, commander of half the chariots, conspired and overthrew the king. There also are two Zimri-das who both defect to the Hebrew cause according to the letters from the Late Bronze Age.

Interim Section Three

THE THIRD GAP
(c. 1300–900 BC)

The story of the West Semites has now been outlined, and in outline it bears a striking resemblance to the narrative compiled in the Hebrew Bible. But if the Hebrew chronicle is the story of the Hebrew-speaking people, who were in Egypt from 2700 BC and in the Levant, Syria and Mesopotamia from 2300 BC, then there is something missing from their chronicle, one vital piece of information which could have been contained in a paragraph, such as:

> Jehosaphat and Zimri died, and all that generation. And the people of Israel were left few in number. And the Lord took delight in bringing ruin upon them and destroying them.
>
> And the time that their enemies oppressed them in the land was more than four hundred years. And after four hundred years Omri began to reign over Israel.

Or:

> In the four-hundred-and-fiftieth year after Jehosaphat and Zimri and all that generation had died, Omri became king. He bought the hill of Samaria and he fortified the hill, and built the city which stands there to this day – a memorial to him.

134

But that is precisely what is missing: a gap. Nothing disappears so easily as a gap. The events to either side of the gap get pushed together, leaving no trace of it. So long as you stick to the rigid chronology provided by the ancient chroniclers, you could go over and over the ground and ·see no sign of a gap.

But if you once relate the fallen walls of Jericho to the subsequent invasion of Western Asia to the Hebrew account of their conquest, then a thousand years after that event, a gap suddenly appears. One short paragraph is missing, and has to be re-inserted.

As with the 400-year period when the Hebrews dwelt in Egypt, and with the 400-year period when the Judges ruled a coalition of Semite powers, so with this third gap in the chronicle, the outside evidence provides some information about this period. The most important piece of information, from the point of view of this study, is that for at least 300 of these years, the whole Ancient Near East fell silent.

Whereas the Bronze Age was a time of prodigious literary activity, the first 300 years of the Iron Age have been called the Dark Ages, from which no literary records survive. It has been debated that the art of writing was lost altogether.

The last event to be recorded in some detail marks the close of the Bronze Age. This was the invasion of the so-called 'Sea Peoples', whose story appears to be the basis of Homer's epics. But it has been argued convincingly that these were not written down until about the eighth century BC, 400 years after the events. In the meanwhile, the ballads were memorized and passed down orally from generation to generation.

The Sea Peoples, moving in fact by land as well as by sea, swept down the whole Eastern Mediterranean coast destroying every city in their path, from Troy to Tyre and on to batter at the very gateway to Egypt, at the mouth of the Nile.

Homer concentrates the action of his *Iliad* around one of these cities only: the one nearest to Greece, of all the cities destroyed at the time. He makes this city the scene of one great siege that lasted many years. But in his second volume, the *Odyssey*, he does tell the story which was supposedly related by a Cretan who had taken part in an expedition that reached the mouth of the Nile. His story appears to tally with the Egyptian account of these events at the close of the Bronze Age.

Here is the Egyptian account:

The foreign countries made a plot in their islands ... and no land could stand before their arms. A camp was set up in one place in Amor, and they desolated its people and its land as though they had never come into being. They came, the flame prepared before them, onwards to Egypt. Their confederacy consisted of (Philistines, the Danoi and others) united lands, and they laid their hands upon the lands to the entire circuit of the earth, their hearts bent and trustful 'Our plan is accomplished!' But the heart of this god, the lord of the gods, was prepared and ready to ensnare them like birds ... I established my boundary, prepared in front of them, the local princes, garrison-commanders, and charioteers. I caused to be prepared the river-mouth like a strong wall with warships, galleys and skiffs. They were completely equipped both fore and aft with brave fighters carrying their weapons and infantry of all the pick of Egypt, being like roaring lions upon the mountains; chariotry with able warriors and all goodly officers whose hands were competent. Their horses quivered in all their limbs, prepared to crush the foreign countries under their hoofs.

As for those who reached my boundary, their seed is not. Their hearts and their souls are finished unto all eternity. Those who came forward together upon the sea, the full flame (of their holocaust) was in front of them at the river-mouths, and a stockade of lances surrounded them on the shore.

A net was prepared for them to ensnare them, those who entered into the river-mouths being confined and fallen within it, pinioned in their places, butchered and their corpses hacked up.[1]

Using the story teller's device, Homer puts into the mouth of Ulysses an episode which would not fit into the tight narrative otherwise. Ulysses was pretending to be a Cretan, which suggests this part of the epic was originally related by a Cretan sailor:

I am a native of the broad lands of Crete, and the son of a wealthy man . . . My glory has departed now, yet I think you will still be able to see by the stubble what the harvest was like . . . in the old days Ares and Athene (God and Goddess of battle) had endowed me generously with the daring that sweeps all before it . . . Anyhow, before the Achaean expedition ever set foot on the coasts of Troy, I had nine times had my own command and led a well-found fleet in a foreign land. As a result, large quantities of plunder fell into my hands . . . Thus my estate increased rapidly and my fellow-countrymen soon learned both to fear and respect me . . . The time came, however, when Zeus, who never takes his eyes off the world, let us in for that deplorable adventure which brought so many men to their knees . . . So for nine years, we Achaeans campaigned at Troy; and after sacking Priam's city in the tenth we sailed for home and our fleet was scattered by a god . . . The spirit moved me to fit out some ships and set sail for Egypt with a picked company. I got nine vessels ready and the crews were soon mustered. For six days my good men gave themselves up to festivity and I provided beasts in plenty for their sacrifices and their own table. On the seventh we embarked, said goodbye to the broad acres of Crete and sailed off with a fresh and favourable wind from the north . . . On the fifth day we reached the great River of Egypt, and there in the Nile I brought my curved ships to . . . The whole place was filled with infantry and chariots and the glint of arms. Zeus the Thunderer struck abject panic into my party. Not a man had the spirit to stand up to the enemy, for we were threatened on all sides. They ended by cutting down a large part of my force and carrying off the survivors to work for them as slaves.

As for myself, a sudden inspiration saved me – though I still wish I had faced my destiny and fallen there in Egypt, for trouble was waiting for me yet with open arms. I quickly doffed my fine helmet, let the shield drop from my shoulder, and threw away my spear. Then I ran up to the king's chariot and embraced his knees. Moved to pity, he spared my life, gave me a seat beside him and so drove his weeping captive home. Many of his people, of course, were lusting for my blood and made at me with their ashen spears, for they were thoroughly roused; but he kept them away, for fear of offending Zeus, the Strangers' god, whose special office it is to call cruelty to account.[2]

So ended the Bronze Age. Silence descended on the Ancient Near East. The first civilization was swept away and mankind was plunged into the Dark Ages. A part of the Sea Peoples were thrown back from Egypt and settled in what became Philistia.

But why did these Sea Peoples suddenly leave their homeland? The evidence suggests that they were displaced by other invaders from further north during the period of the violent expansion of the Celtic races who conquered the world from Ireland to India. Their warriors were mounted on horseback for the first time, and had iron weapons. They were invincible.

It is possible that Jerusalem alone held out, like a booth

in a vineyard, and that the Hebrew chroniclers did preserve a brief and fearful account of this period.

For the eyes of the Lord move to and fro throughout the whole earth, ... from now on you will have wars.[3]

The Lord will bring a nation against you from afar, from the end of the earth, as swift as the eagle flies, a nation whose language you do not understand, a nation of stern countenance, who shall not regard the person of the old or show favour to the young, and shall eat the offspring of your cattle and the fruit of your ground, until you are destroyed; who also shall not leave you grain, wine or oil, the increase of your cattle or the young of your flock, until they have caused you to perish. They shall besiege you in all your towns until your high and fortified walls, in which you trusted, come down throughout all your land; and they shall besiege you in all your towns throughout all your land, which the Lord your God, has given you. And you shall eat the offspring of your own body, the flesh of your sons and daughters, whom the Lord your God has given you, in the siege and in the distress with which your enemies shall distress you. The man who is the most tender and delicately bred among you will grudge food to his brother, to the wife of his bosom and to the last of the children who remain to him; so that he will not give to any of them any of the flesh of his children whom he is eating, because he has nothing left him, in the siege and in the distress with which your enemy shall distress you in all your towns. The most tender and delicately bred woman among you, who would not venture to set the sole of her foot upon the ground because she is so delicate and tender, will grudge to the husband of her bosom, to her son and to her daughter, her afterbirth that comes out from between her feet and her children whom she bears, because she will eat them secretly, for want of all things, in the siege and in the distress with which your enemy shall distress you in your towns.[4]

═══ 5 ═══

THE CHRONICLERS

The Swan-song

From the reign of King Omri to the fall of Jerusalem there was a period of partial and limited recovery for the Hebrew-speaking people before their final eclipse. It is as if the Hebrews as a people were wiped from the face of the earth at the end of the Bronze Age. They are never again mentioned in outside records by the name Habiru or Hebrew, the old spelling or the new.

In their place are the People of Israel, one small section of a once-great northern state – the single state of Old Assur with its port on the coast of Tyre, now splintered into three: Assyria, Syria and Ysra-el. Just as the Hebrews are mentioned for the very last time, so Ysra-el is mentioned for the very first time, by the Pharaoh Merneptah whose reign marked the end of the New Empire and the close of the Bronze Age.

Then the curtain fell. The long silence of the Dark Ages followed. When the curtain rose again, it rose on a very different world. For a while, there were the little kingdom of Israel and the little kingdom of Judah, until Israel, with its new capital at Samaria, fell. Then, the remaining people of Israel fled south into Judah, with its capital at Jerusalem. Then Jerusalem fell.

Israel fell to Sargon II, and the new Assyrian Empire.

Jerusalem fell to Nebuchadnezzer and the New Babylonian Empire. But not long after that, both fell to the Medes, the Persians and then to the Greeks.

Out of the People of Israel were born the Jews, whose everyday language became Aramaic. The People of Israel in Judah had compiled and edited their magnificent swan-song, the Bible. They were also lucky. Like every other nation around them they were trying to retrieve their past, to discover their roots. And it was in this connection that they had a lucky find when repairing their megalithic temple.

Behind the Megalithic Stones of the Temple Walls

Samaria had already fallen and the Hebrew-speaking people had little left to them except Jerusalem and its immediate surrounds. They were a beleaguered people in a city whose outer ramparts dated back to the Late Bronze Age, and whose temple was a typical Bronze Age structure.

It was behind such walls as those which form the so-called 'Wailing Wall' in Jerusalem that a manuscript was found in the reign of King Josiah (640–609 BC). In the eighteenth year of Josiah, the king sent Shaphan and the governor of the city and the recorder to repair the house of the Lord his God. They came to the high priest and delivered the money which the keepers of the threshold had collected from the remnant of Israel and from all Judah and from the inhabitants of Jerusalem. They gave it to the carpenters and builders to buy quarried stone and timber for the buildings which the kings of Judah had let go to ruin.

> And Hilkiah the high priest said to Shaphan the secretary, 'I have found the book of the law in the house of the Lord.' And Hilkiah gave the book to Shaphan, and he read it . . . Then Shaphan the secretary told the king, 'Hilkiah the priest has given me a book.' And Shaphan read it before the king.

And when the king heard the words of the book of the law, he rent his clothes. And the king commanded Hilkiah the priest and Achiam the son of Shaphan the secretary and Achbor the son of Micaiah, and Shaphan the secretary, and Asaiah the king's servant, saying, 'Go, inquire of the Lord for me, and for the people, and for all Judah, concerning the words of this book that has been found; for great is the wrath of the Lord that is kindled against us, because our fathers have not obeyed the words of this book, to do according to all that is written concerning us.' . . .

Then the king sent, and all the elders of Judah and Jerusalem were gathered to him. And the king went up to the house of the Lord, and with him all the men of Judah, and all the inhabitants of Jerusalem, and the priests and prophets, all the people, both small and great; and he read in their hearing all the words of the book of the covenant which had been found in the house of the Lord. And the king stood by the pillar and made a covenant before the Lord, to walk after the Lord and to keep his commandments and his testimonies and his statutes, with all his heart and all his soul, to perform the words of this covenant that were written in this book; and all the people joined in the covenant.

And the king commanded Hilkiah the high priest, and the priests of the second order, and the keepers of the threshold, to bring out of the temple of the Lord all the vessels made for Baal, for Asherah and for all the host of heaven, he burned them outside Jerusalem in the fields of the Kidron, and carried their ashes to Bethel. And he deposed the idolatrous priests whom the kings of Judah had ordered to burn incense to Baal, to the sun, and the moon, and the constellations, and all the host of the heavens. And he brought out the Asherah from the house of the Lord, outside Jerusalem, to the brook Kidron and burned it at the brook Kidron and beat it to dust and cast the dust of it upon the graves of the common people . . .

And he removed the horses that the kings of Judah had dedicated to the sun, at the entrance of the house of the Lord, . . . and he burned the chariots of the sun with fire. And the king defiled the high places that were east of Jerusalem, to the south of the mount of corruption, which Solomon the king of Israel had built for Ashtoreth the abomination of the Sidonians and for Chemosh the abomination of Moab, and for Milcom the abomination of the Ammonites. And he broke in pieces the pillars, and cut down the Asherim, and filled their places with the bones of men.

And he slew all the priests of the high places who were there, upon the altars and burned the bones of men upon them. Then he returned to Jerusalem.

And the king commanded all the people, 'Keep the passover of the Lord your God, as it is written in this book of the covenant.' For no such passover had been kept since the days of the judges . . . but in the eighteenth year of King Josiah this passover was kept to the Lord in Jerusalem.[1]

An earlier wave of religious reform had not only broken the pillars and cut down the Asherah, but it also:

broke in pieces the bronze serpent that Moses had made, for until those days the people of Israel had burned incense to it.[2]

This suggests that the sweeping reforms of this period were not strictly in accordance with the 'law of the Lord given through Moses'.

Moreover Josiah put away the mediums and the wizards and the teraphim.[3]

And his prophet Jeremiah preached a new covenant in place
of the old:

> Behold, the days are coming, says the Lord, when I will
> make a new covenant with the house of Israel and the
> house of Judah, not like the covenant which I made
> with their fathers when I took them by the hand to bring
> them out of the land of Egypt, my covenant which they
> broke . . .
>
> So do not listen to your prophets, your diviners, your
> dreamers, your soothsayers, or your sorcerers . . .
>
> How long shall there be lies in the heart of the prophets
> who prophesy lies . . . who think to make my people for-
> get my name by their dreams which they tell one another,
> even as their fathers forgot my name for Baal? . . . Behold,
> I am against those who prophesy lying dreams.
>
> Then all the men . . . answered Jeremiah: 'As for the
> word which you have spoken to us in the name of the
> Lord, we will not listen to you. But we will do every-
> thing that we have vowed, burn incense to the queen
> of heaven and pour out libations to her, as we did,
> both we and our fathers, our kings and our princes,
> in the cities of Judah and in the streets of Jerusalem;
> for then we had plenty of food, and prospered, and
> saw no evil. But since we left off burning incense to
> the queen of heaven and pouring out libations to her,
> we have lacked everything and have been consumed
> by the sword and by famine.' And the women said,
> 'When we burned incense to the queen of heaven
> and poured out libations to her, was it without our
> husband's approval that we made cakes for her bearing
> her image and poured out libations to her?'[4]

That is enough to give some idea of the political and religious conditions in which the Hebrew chroniclers were
working.

But if Julian Jaynes is right, there had also been a profound psychological change: the mythological mentality

was something of the past, and the modern logical mentality had taken its place. The religious reforms inevitably reflected this psychological change.

The chroniclers of the Modern Era must have had access to material that included a detailed biography dating from the beginning of the Pyramid Age, a vivid account of the collapse of the Pyramid Age, an accurate chronicle of the invasion of the Levant at the end of the early Bronze Age and a well-documented history of the West Semite empire that was crushed and plundered in the fifteenth century BC. I can't help thinking that the Book of the Law which the high priest found at the time when extensive repairs were being made to the ruins of the ancient temple must have contained a large proportion of this extraordinary material. No other document from the Hebrew-speaking people of the Early and Middle Bronze Age has survived.

By some extraordinary chance this particular wealth of material was preserved. We know that works comparable with the Bible were compiled in the Bronze Age. There was, for example, the so-called 'Hammurabi Bible' about which we know a little although it has not survived. It contained genealogies, a mythological section and an historical section, and comparisons have been made between it and the Hebrew Bible. There was also a Phoenician version. In my opinion, at the time when the West Semite empire stretched across the Near East, the three different versions of Semite history had already been worked into a single narrative which survived by an unlikely chance the ravages which swept so much Bronze Age literature into oblivion. Mycenean Greece, Minoan Crete, the Hittites, the kingdom of Ugarit with its sixty great cities, the kingdoms of Alalakh and Ebla, the empire of Sumer and Agade were all gone, leaving only faint traces of their existence until they were rediscovered recently by the painstaking work of archaeologists.

For me, the most likely explanation for the survival of this material is described in the detail it deserves, as the great event of King Josiah's reign.

The Hebrew Chroniclers Themselves

However, if the chief sources of the chroniclers' material was from the Bronze Age, as previously suggested, then we know something of the type of material they were working from, and also something of the extent to which they revised and reworked that material in order to make it satisfy the psychological, political and religious situation in their own time.

I have often tried to imagine them at work in the library of King Josiah. Would they be lifting down clay letters, answers from the Pharaoh Akhenaten to their ancestors? Would some of them be out on the streets trying to gather all the old stories, passed down orally from generation to generation? Just as there were at least five Pythagorases who contributed to the teaching of Pythagoras, in the same way, many oracles from very different periods of time have been collected in the Oracles of Isaiah.

From the evidence of the Bible itself, the chief source material had been preserved in the form of ritual: the rubrics and ceremonial words of ritual, preserved in an annual cycle of festivals and celebrations. This is not a guess. It is the nature of the book even to this day and it is used mainly in this way. There are instructions throughout the book that it should be so used.

Such a book may provide an abundant source of history, but there are drawbacks if you treat it as a history. If you try to imagine reconstructing the history of the Catholic Church from the Roman Catholic Missal, you could begin to get an idea of the problems confronting the scribes and chroniclers in the seventh century BC.

Whether you accept the speculation that an important and extensive Bronze Age Bible was found preserved in some hidden cache in the temple or not, the fact remains that the chroniclers working in the seventh century to recover the history of their people would have had very little difficulty retrieving the past two centuries as far back as Omri. The city that he founded, his capital Samaria, had fallen to the Assyrians, almost within living memory.

But when they reached *c.* 900 BC and tried to look back beyond that, they would have been faced with very grave difficulties indeed. They would have been standing on the edge of the Dark Ages, peering into the obscurity. If Kathleen Kenyon has done her painstaking archaeological work as accurately and successfully as it would appear from all her careful stratification, then they would have been staring into a long period of extreme poverty in which there was no trade, the country was thinly populated, and the magnificent civilization of the Bronze Age had, mostly, already sunk beneath mounds of grass.

I think the chroniclers did get some vague picture of this period: but they didn't have any idea of the length of it. They have fragments of knowledge only:

Hark, an uproar of kingdoms, of nations gathering . . .[5]

We get glimpses of how these nations swooped and destroyed city after city. For example, Gilead which, like Ugarit in the Bronze Age, was combined with sixty other great cities with walls and bronze bars, lay in ruins:

You are as Gilead to me, as the summit of Lebanon, yet surely I will make you a desert, an uninhabited city. I will prepare destroyers against you, each with his weapons; and they shall cut down your choicest cedars and cast them into the fire.[6]

And:

'. . . behold, here come riders, horsemen in pairs . . . from the uttermost parts of the North, . . . against the mountains of Israel.

I will send fire on . . . those who dwell secure in the coastlands . . .

The Lord of hosts is mustering a host for battle. They come from a distant land . . . to destroy the whole earth. Whoever is found will be thrust through and whoever is caught will fall by the sword. Their infants will be dashed in pieces before their eyes; their houses will be plundered and their wives ravished; their cities burned with fire.

Gog, of the land of Magog, the chief prince of Meshech and Tubal, ... Gomer and all his hordes ... and all (his) army, horses and horsemen, all of them clothed in full armour, a great company, all of them with buckler and shield, wielding swords; Persia, Cush and Put are with them.[7]

Only with hindsight, knowing what happened at the end of the Bronze Age, would you notice these little fragments, wonder about them and piece them together. The names all refer to the sons of Japheth, the Indo-European races whose mounted cavalry conquered the world from Ireland to India at the close of the Bronze Age. The chroniclers themselves did not manage to preserve any such coherent picture of the Dark Ages that lay between the end of the Bronze Age and their own time.

As a result, they joined the recent past, the last 200 years, directly onto the last surviving records which were transmitted to them by one way or another from the Bronze Age. For example, episodes from the reigns of Jehosaphat and Zimri and before that Asa, and before him Abijah, which seem to correspond with incidents that occurred much earlier as described in the correspondence with the Pharaoh Akhenaten. Thereby, kings who reigned in the ninth century BC are, by mistake, made the direct successors of kings who had reigned towards the end of the fourteenth century BC.

The chroniclers lost 400 years of their story. Once these 400 years are restored and the earlier part of the story is set side by side with Bronze Age history as we now know it, then a picture of remarkable clarity emerges – but it is a picture very different from the one commonly accepted at the moment.

149

Interim Section Four

THE FOURTH GAP
(586–166 BC)

The fourth gap is not strictly speaking part of my story, because it took place after the end of the Bronze Age and the chroniclers' narrative. I include it here, nevertheless, because it illustrates how and why the chroniclers could and did leave out large chunks of their story, not just in the beginning but also at the end of it. This makes it all the more probable that they could have left a similar gap, in similar circumstances, right in the middle of their story.

As with the third gap, the chroniclers make no mention of this fourth gap, which might also have disappeared without trace, except that it covers four centuries that are comparatively well known to us, and include the reign of Alexander the Great.

None the less, the chroniclers fail to mention it, possibly for exactly the same reason as they failed to mention the third gap, because there were no courts, no kings and so no regnal years. So the centuries passed uncounted.

Even right at the end of their story, when several generations of Jewish chroniclers were already engaged on the great work of presenting a history of their people, a vital bit still got left out. It could have been summed up in one sentence, such as:

In the four hundred and twentieth year after the

150

Babylonian king had burned the House of God, and broken down the walls of Jerusalem, Judas Maccabeus took unhewn stones, as the law directs, and built a new altar.

Or:

All those who escaped the sword were taken into exile in Babylon, and after that four hundred and twenty years elapsed, before Judas Maccabeus took command in Israel.

But that is precisely what is missing: one sentence accounting for a gap of several hundred years.

The events to either side of this gap might have got pushed together, and closed over the gap, leaving little trace of it. But once you relate the Jewish history to the history of the surrounding nations, the gap inevitably appears.

In his *History of Israel*, John Bright writes of these centuries:

Our biblical sources are at best inadequate. We are presented with many gaps that must be filled in, as far as possible. Toward the end of the fifth century (BC) the historical narrative of the Bible stops altogether; not until the second century . . . may Jewish historical sources be said to resume. When all is done, dismaying lacunae and baffling problems remain.

And the situation of the West Semites between 1300–900 BC was almost identical with that of the Jews between 600–200 BC: in both periods the Hebrew-speaking people had been dominated by foreign powers and deported in large numbers.

151

MY CONCLUSIONS CONCERNING THE FACTS BEHIND THE MYTH

The Short Chronology (1700–700 BC)

For a long time, one small omission on the part of the ancient Hebrew chroniclers didn't make much difference. it didn't really matter whether Joseph lived in 1700 BC or 2700 BC. For more than 2,500 years nobody knew enough about the Bronze Age for it to make any difference, one way or the other. But in the last forty years or so, that small scribal error has caused havoc with the chronologies of the Ancient Near East.

When Professor Garstang found the very ancient walls of Jericho, he naturally assumed that there was some connection between these walls and the story of the walls of Jericho falling down for the benefit of Joshua's army in Hebrew tradition. So did everyone else for a while. It became part of the textbook version of history. But not for long. Kathleen Kenyon carried out a more carefully stratified archaeological dig and showed conclusively that the walls fell nearly a thousand years earlier than Professor Garstang had thought.

Nobody thought to question the chronology of the Hebrew chroniclers, in spite of the fact that none of their contemporaries had ever had a reliable chronology

(Ashurbanapal, Herodotus, Manetho etc.). The point is that there was no firm date in the whole of the Ancient World. The main way of calculating the years was by counting the number of years a king reigned and adding up the reigns. But this led to two kinds of confusion: when there were two kings of the south and north of Egypt, for example, their reigns often got added one after the other, which made some periods excessively long. There were other periods when there were no kings (or judges) and such periods were inclined to get unnaturally foreshortened. Nevertheless, the chronology of the Bible remained axiomatic, sacrosanct. And this has remained the textbook version of Ancient History, though it is just beginning to be challenged.

This textbook version I will call the Short Chronology: 1700–700 BC.

Of course if there were some compelling reasons for adhering to this late chronology, then that would be that. But there don't appear to be any such compelling reasons. In fact this late dating of all the Hebrew material has presented nothing but problems, for which very far-fetched solutions had to be found.

The only thing which at first glance seems to be in favour of the late dates, is that they place so much of the Hebrew story in the Dark Ages, so that there is no evidence from outside documents to refute it. But there is nothing to corroborate it either, because there are no documents. This is convenient in one way because it leaves the Hebrew story in a little vacuum bubble on its own. But to me it is totally unacceptable that, just when the rest of the Ancient Near East fell silent and records ceased, the Hebrew scribes alone were busy. And it doesn't take outside written documents to show that the result of their endeavours was a work of pure fiction, if the empire of David and Solomon is set in the context of the Dark Ages, the abysmal period between 1200 and 900 BC. We shall return to that.

First, let's start with Joseph and try to see if there is anything which irrevocably links his story with the late date of 1700 BC. There was no known vizier who in any way corresponds to him, but that is not to be expected, perhaps. This was the beginning of the period of the foreign rulers (the Hyksos) in Egypt, who have been positively identified by Manetho, the Egyptian chronicler, with the ancestors of the Jews inhabiting Jerusalem and Judaea. So far so good. But Manetho is also categorical that Moses lived 518 years before the Pharaoh Amenophis chased the foreign rulers out of Egypt and pursued them as far as Syria. Josephus repeats this 518 year gap between Moses and the foreign rulers three times. But what is more significant still is that the foreign rulers arrived as a conquering army and crowned their first king. This has nothing in common with the story of Joseph and his brothers. The period is convenient only in the sense that Avaris, the capital of the foreign rulers, was destroyed by the Pharaohs and has never been excavated; and later Pharaohs attempted to erase all trace of the occupation of Egypt by the Asiatics from their records. So the Hebrew story is not volubly contradicted.

From there the Hebrew story skips 400 years to the Plagues, and the Exodus, and scholars have been puzzled why these dramatic events went completely unnoticed by the Egyptians in a period which was otherwise so well documented. It would be unreasonable to expect a small band of tribesmen (for that is the way the textbook version depicts the Hebrews in the wilderness, both in pictures and in words) to leave any trace of their wandering in the desert. But the conquest is another matter. You would expect to find some trace of the newly arrived population in the archaeological record. However there isn't any such trace, so an explanation must be found instead.

The commonly accepted explanation is that the Hebrews 'infiltrated' into the land, huddled under the walls of the great cities and in due course made some kind of an 'ideological' conquest, rather in the manner of the Christians emerging from the catacombs to take Rome in the time of Constantine – a comparison which has already been made. A ghost army that leaves no footprints. Fantasian forces tripping over the bricks at Jericho, that had been lying there a thousand years, passing the mound that already covered the ruins of Ai, which had never been rebuilt after the earlier nomadic invasion, and gliding into the hills, before they could drop any pottery that might be identified. A desultory attempt has been made to link this fantasian invasion with the Habiru chiefs who were menacing the regents of the Pharaoh Akhenaten at the time. But the Habiru chiefs were also regents and viceroys of the Pharaoh and in correspondence with him, which is an unlikely background for the Exodus and Conquest. And in any case, leaving Egypt to re-enter another part of the Egyptian Empire is at odds with the story as preserved by Hebrew tradition. It is true that there were a few towns burned at this period, but what period is free of that? We do, however, know perfectly well who was responsible: the punitive expeditions of the Pharaohs against their West Semite enemies, and internal strife between the indigenous West Semites and the foreign occupation viceroys with their forces, as described in the letters to Akhenaten.

Finally, we come to the magnificent Empire of Saul, David and Solomon, set in its late context at the nadir of the Dark Ages. The great trading ships that were away three years, apparently returned empty, all the tribute from the kings of the earth had vanished. Kathleen Kenyon can't find trace of a single imported object for this period. The Empire seems to have reached not much further than the suburbs of Jerusalem. But all this can be explained: it is the weakness of Assyria and the weakness of Egypt at the same time that gave the Hebrews a momentary illusion of grandeur. And that's when they started scribbling prodigiously in their garrets, just when everybody else had stopped, and so couldn't write anything to contradict them.

I don't think so.

A Note: Early and Late
If the Hebrews were in the Levant throughout the Middle

Bronze Age, they were also there in the Iron Age. Just because some of the material in the Hebrew Chronicle most definitely refers to the late period, this cannot be used as an argument to prove the late chronology, as has been done. It is not a question of either/or, but both/and.

There is plenty of proof that the people of Israel were in the Levant by the beginning of the Iron Age, but added to this there is plenty of evidence that the Hebrews were already there a thousand years earlier, and that the people of Israel were merely the surviving portion of this much larger West Semite or Hebrew-speaking people.

A thousand years is added to the story. And throughout this thousand-year period there is no significant break in the culture: there is no evidence of any new arrivals, or any important new ingredient in the population. The same people, making consistently developing pottery forms within the same tradition, speaking the same language (Hebrew) with the same rituals etc. inhabited the Levant from the beginning of the Middle Bronze Age – 2100 BC – right up to the time when 'Israel' is mentioned for the first time by the Pharaoh Merneptah. All the archaeological evidence points to continuous occupation by the same stable population. But because the Israelites had to get there sometime, if you don't consider that they are the nomads who invaded in 2300 BC, then another invasion has to be invented for a later date, contrary to all the evidence, ignoring the evidence. It is a purely fictitious hypothetical invasion that flies in the face of the evidence.

The Long Chronology: 2700–700 BC
Striking parallels with the Bronze Age, from which large portions of the entire Bible have now been recovered.

By contrast with the late chronology, the early dating plus the gap, as outlined in Part Two of this book, is packed with corroborative evidence of every kind which I shall endeavour to condense into the following pages.

The evidence I have produced is not a matter of little minor academic points into which only I have delved. What I am talking about are the major events of the Bronze Age and its most prominent figures, compared to and correlated with the major events of the Hebrew story and its most prominent figures.

It is not only me who has noticed these comparisons. Almost every single one has been noticed by an eminent scholar in the field. You can't help noticing them. But one of the difficulties for modern scholarship, is that each expert works in a particular field, and it is only when you put all these fields together that you can notice the weight of accumulative evidence. I have taken up the task of gathering the fruit of all this expertise and presenting it to the best of my ability. With no particular expertise of my own, which would otherwise absorb all my time and attention, I am able to make a synthesis of the whole.

I don't know how familiar Wallis Budge was with the Bible, but with only a schoolchild's knowledge, you are inevitably struck by the comparison of a seven-year famine in the time of Imhotep, and a seven-year famine in the story of Joseph. And Wallis Budge was duly struck by it and noted it in the introduction to his translation of the text. I think he was too absorbed in deciphering hieroglyphs and in his fascinating studies of Egyptology to bother to open his Bible again, or he would have been even more struck by the many other parallels between the two stories, as I was.

Velikovsky was struck by the extraordinary parallels between the Ipuwer papyrus and the Hebrew account of the plagues. Unlike Wallis Budge, he didn't leave it at that, but pioneered the whole idea of revising the chronology. For this reason, he has been a major influence behind my work. His *Ages in Chaos* came out in 1952, shortly before Kathleen Kenyon redated the walls of Jericho. If the two events could have been related at the same time we might have avoided decades, not to mention volumes, of confusion.

When I started these researches the last thing I expected was to find any traces of the period the Hebrews spent in the wilderness. So I was very surprised when I first read Nelson Glueck, who discovered a freak occupation of the Negeb at the end of Early Bronze Age. The Hebrew trek across the wilderness between Egypt and the Levant had left its indelible mark which is there to this day, to be interpreted and reinterpreted. Now in the capable hands of Professor Cohen and Professor Anati, it is this evidence which is beginning to make an impression in scholarly circles, and may in due course necessitate the earlier dating: the long chronology. In the hands of Cohen and Anati it has become the cornerstone for reconsidering the dates. The new evidence in their capable hands has aroused the curiosity of the academic establishment as well as of the public.

Professor Garstang was struck by the fallen walls around Jericho, and so was the world. After Jericho, Joshua attacked and destroyed Ai. And this has always been a bugbear to archaeologists and Biblical scholars, because the only time when Ai was destroyed was at the end of the Early Bronze Age. It was never rebuilt, in order to be burned again at a more convenient time. W. E. Albright was so struck by this that he suggested, more than fifty years ago, that a description of the original destruction of Ai in 2300 BC must have got included in the Hebrew narrative. He was very influential at the time and it is a pity he didn't go on to think that the original episode of the tumbling walls of Jericho might have also got included, as well as the rest of the subsequent invasion, especially since he was in correspondence with Velikovsky and so could have entertained the notion of querying the accepted late chronology.

Introducing the texts from Ancient Ugarit, John Gray writes: 'In principal and often in detail there are striking correspondences with Hebrew life and culture.' In his book, *The Canaanites*, which is another name for the Old Phoenicians, and in Cyrus Gordon's *Before the Bible*, both point out copious comparisons between the West Semites in the Middle Bronze Age, and the Hebrews in the same area but allegedly much later. If you put together their comparisons in literature, customs, language, laws, psalms, feasts, proverbs etc. with my comparisons as outlined in previous chapters you will find it true to say that almost everything in the Bible has been found (albeit in fragments) in parallel texts from the Bronze Age. J. B. Pritchard's *Ancient Near Eastern Texts* and D. Winton Thomas's *Documents from Old Testament Times* have compiled some of these texts, which in language and style, as well as content, can be compared with similar material in the Hebrew account.

For example, John Gray is so struck by the parallels between Yassib, the son of Keret, and Absalom, the son of David, that he calls Yassib the Canaanite Absalom.

In his history of Palestine and Syria, A. T. Olmstead is so struck by the wealth of this area in the Late Bronze Age when Pharaoh Tuthmosis plundered it, that he calls it 'legendary' and compares it to the legendary wealth of Solomon. Kathleen Kenyon, concentrating on the archaeological record alone, does not find evidence of this great wealth, although I would have thought the prodigious building schemes alone would have suggested it.

Nevertheless, in spite of having observed all these striking parallels and comparisons, the late chronology had never been seriously questioned by the academic establishment until Professor Anati produced new archaeological evidence of an overwhelming nature.

The superstructure of the short chronology has dominated the thinking of several generations of scholars. Yet it is far from adamantine. It rests on very flimsy evidence indeed.

But there has been one advantage arising from the fact that the standard version of history has clung rigidly to the late chronology. It does mean that all the striking parallels exist in their own right, and aren't there because anybody has tried to fit the Bronze Age material together with the Hebrew Chronicle. They are stark. And now they can be related, with a fresh mind, all at once. But they will always exist now in their own right too.

All the publications before Professor Anati's *Mountain of God* (1986) are there now, for anyone who wants to see what the material looked like before it was correlated with the biblical material.

These two phases of the work (whereby each part has preserved its separate identity and can now be related) seem especially valuable and meaningful in relation to the Old Religion behind our living religions: the myth behind the facts.

PART THREE

The Myth
Behind the Facts

The Shattered Myth

The particular contribution of this study is to identify the ancient Hebrews with the West Semites, Old Phoenicians, and Akkadians in the Bronze Age. But the study would not be complete without looking at the relationship between the oldest strata of Hebrew religion – hidden beneath later reforms and discernible between the lines only – and the religion of those Semites in the Bronze Age in Mesopotamia, Egypt and the Levant.

If the Hebrews left Ur with the rise of the Sumerian city states in around 2850 BC and were established in the Delta region of Egypt for the 400 years of the Pyramid Age, then it was they who introduced, or at least revered, the gods of the Semite Provinces who were investigated with imaginative scholarship by George Aaron Barton at the beginning of this century: Semite gods such as Ptah, Osiris, Ra, etc. Similarly, if the Hebrew tribes were the Semites of the Levant and Mesopotamia in the ensuing Middle Bronze Age then there must be some relationship between the ancient cult of these areas and the religion of the old Hebrews.

For me, the connection lies in the zodiac – not horoscopes originally, but the ancient calendar or cycle of the year, animated by celestial beasts. My investigations have led me to the conviction that this was the old cult throughout the ancient world and was held in common by the whole of the Bronze Age civilization. But the worrying question immediately arises, if there was this single myth, held in common by all mankind throughout the Age of Myth and possibly long before, then why isn't there more evidence of it? Why didn't we know about it before?

This book has been telling the story of a civilization that was fragmented and destroyed more than 3,000 years ago. Until Schliemann dug up Troy in 1871, people hardly believed in its reality. We have only just begun to rediscover it. The evidence is necessarily meagre and the hard facts are few and far between.

When the Bronze Age civilization was fragmented, I think its myth was shattered also. Just as the civilization was once a single inter-related whole, so there was a single myth held in common. When this myth is reconstructed it makes sense of many isolated fragments that are incomprehensible otherwise, although there are, however, two special factors which should be taken into account.

As with other Bronze Age material most of the evidence has been destroyed, but in the case of the myth, conspicuous by their absence from the rubble of the Bronze Age are the ceilings of its temples – not a single ceiling has survived. We know from later ceilings in classical times, that the ceiling was the traditional (as well as the obvious) place to depict the celestial myth based on the zodiac: for example, the ceiling of the Temple at Denderah in Egypt, or the beautiful zodiac mosaic on the ceiling of the Jewish synagogue at Beth Shan (second century AD). Traditionally, Semite temples, like later Christian churches, faced east, and the six dark signs of the zodiac would be placed on the left and northern half of the ceiling, often with a door in the centre of this northern side, representing midwinter: the Janus Door. Many Christian cathedrals still follow this pattern, long after the celestial significance has been forgotten. Even in the rare instances where the rest of a Bronze Age temple has survived, the ceiling has not as, after all, the first part of any edifice to fall is the ceiling. It is a negative argument, but all the same it does explain how the bulk of the evidence came to be annihilated.

The second factor to take into consideration is equally negative. In later classical times, there seems to have been a sweeping reaction against the old cult which has contributed to a further erosion of the evidence. It wasn't just the Hebrew kings and prophets who railed against the cult of the high places and the stars, but in Egypt also Budge suggests that later scribes have tampered with the text of *The Egyptian Book of the Dead*. As a result, there are chapters where the pictures suggest the zodiac, but the text reads as if it comes from a degenerate period of religion when talismans and formulas, bought at a price, were all that was left. In particular, it would appear that the later Egyptian priesthood was unable to grasp the complex and exacting astronomy that underpinned the myth.

As a result of these two factors, the evidence which has survived is especially meagre, and I have ranged far afield to collect what fragments there are at present. But the different pieces do appear to fit the same overall framework and all point towards a single universal myth. But above all, the myths themselves take on new significance in the light of this one myth, and tend to substantiate what other evidence there is. In the light of the zodiac they tell a tale which could have been understood by anyone at the time. And in relation to this myth, we can discern an underlying Hebrew myth, along the same lines which is, in turn, the source of the Christian sacred cycle of the year to this day.

My main point in the following sections is to display what evidence there is for an overall structure and pattern to myth in the Age of Myth, based on the calendar and the zodiac and further to show the extent to which Hebrew myth and religion conformed to the Bronze Age pattern.

7

ONE UNIVERSAL MYTH

Worldwide

There has been a lot of wild speculation about what became of the lost tribes of the House of Israel after the break up of Solomon's Empire, when ten tribes were torn from the hands of his descendants. Some have found traces of them in northern Europe, others have claimed them for the Americas, and yet others have spotted them in India. I think they may all be right.

At first it seemed quite a small thing to identify the Hebrews with the ancient West Semites, or Hebrew-speaking peoples, inhabiting the Ancient Near East in the Bronze Age. However, if you combine the archaeological picture of this period (especially the twenty-seventh to the fifteenth centuries BC) with the picture that emerges from the Bible you will see some extraordinary results which are not easy to dismiss.

This period of high civilization in the Near East coincides with a period of global activity, and there have been many attempts to link the two. One obvious, striking image of the possibility that the two may be linked is the flat-topped pyramids called ziggurats in Mesopotamia, and the flat-topped pyramids of the Mayan civilization in the Americas. But as we saw, this was also the design of the altar in Solomon's temple, as described by Ezekiel, albeit in miniature.

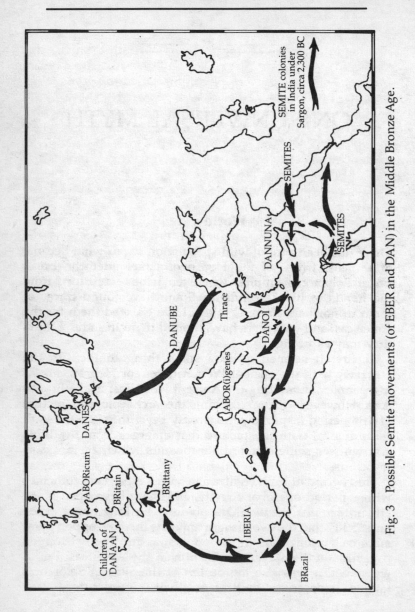

Fig. 3 Possible Semite movements (of EBER and DAN) in the Middle Bronze Age.

This is one instance of a mass of accumulating data on the interchange of ideas, crops, breeding stock, etc., between the Ancient Near East and the Americas before 1492 BC, 3,000 years before Columbus sailed the ocean. Very recently, in 1989, Gene Savoy was reported to have found Semitic hieroglyphs in a lost Peruvian jungle city, which suggest that Peru was the Ophir where Solomon went for his gold, and add one more piece to the mass of convincing evidence already collected by Professor Cyrus Gordon in his book *Before Columbus*.

This possibility becomes all the more probable if the Semite powers of the Ancient Near East formed a tight coalition and were ultimately forged into a single empire. If you separate the Egyptians from the Mesopotamians, the Mesopotamians from the inhabitants of the Levant, and the West Semites from the Mycenean Greeks and the Cretans, then it hardly seems possible that any one of them could have changed the face of the earth in the particular way it was changed during this period . . . But if these powers had ever been united, as Part Two of this study suggests, then their combined forces would have been truly formidable. Compare the united forces of Islam conquering Spain and battering at the gates of Vienna, thus threatening all Europe some 2,400 years later.

But the new perspective on the West Semite empire of David and Solomon suggests just this: they would have been able to draw on the resources of Agade (Gad) and Old Assyria (Asher), as well as the powerful state of Dannuna (Dan); also Mycenean Greece (The Danoi) and Minoan Crete (where the 'Dawida' was chief, linking with David's personal bodyguard of Cretans). Plus the resources of the Old Phoenicians with their renowned navigational skills, and the expertise of northern Egypt where they had their summer capital at Avaris.

Surely the combined forces of the united Semite race – which included many other vital racial ingredients such as Sumerians, Hurrians and Mitanni, each with special skills

– could have reached 'the ends of the earth' (*Deuteronomy* 33/17) in their heyday during the Bronze Age.

Somebody did. Somebody built the megaliths in this period, and carried the zodiac to the ends of the earth. And because of the technical expertise and the unity of the Semites at the time, it is more likely to have been them than anyone else. Furthermore, the chroniclers of a later time have preserved beliefs that the descendants of Abraham would go to the ends of the earth, and that Solomon's ships were away for three years. It is especially such skills as transporting and raising huge obelisks, building domes, and the navigational skills required, that suggest the Ancient Near East where, for example, ocean-worthy vessels were already depicted inside the pyramids, and the Old Phoenicians were already shipping timber to Egypt.

Who else is there as a candidate for constructing the megaliths, building Stonehenge? Who else had the technology to build the extraordinary domed structures along the peaks of Bodmin Moor in Cornwall, England? Who on earth had the incentive to transport and align the massive stones at Carnac, Brittany? If it wasn't the Semites who erected megaliths in the valley south of Jerusalem, who aligned stones at the foot of Mount Sinai and built a circle of stones as their first act on entering the new land promised to their forefathers, then who was it? Their own chronicle almost begins with erecting such a stone to commemorate Jacob's dream of a ladder connecting Heaven and Earth: Jacob's Ladder.

The fragments of evidence are there, and new bits get added, but they are yet to be interpreted. For me the most important piece of evidence is the dates. All this global activity coincides very precisely with the rise of Semites in Mesopotamia and Egypt, then in western Asia, with their very special technological skills which included astronomy. And then, with the fall of the West Semites, all the global activity of building megaliths and other cyclopean structures terminates abruptly.

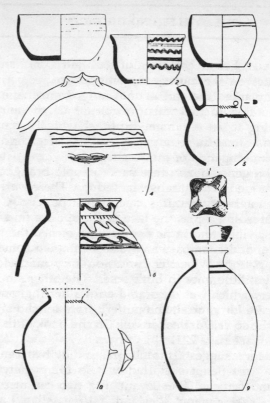

Fig. 4   Pottery of the Middle Bronze Age from Jericho.

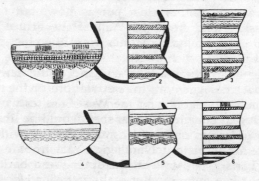

Fig. 5   Maritime Beaker pottery from Central Portugal.

In particular, I can't help thinking of half a million foot-loose Semites on the move out of Egypt in the period of hiatus that marked the end of the Early Bronze Age. Half a million battle-hardened warriors going back to their tents and returning to an old nomadic ideal which gave them mobility and strength, toughened by the fierce conditions of that freak occupation of the Negeb.

For several generations these same people brought their dead to be buried in the tombs near Jericho. These were large individual tombs containing distinctive pottery. Coincidentally, spreading across the face of Europe we find traces of a highly civilized nomadic people who buried their dead in large individual tombs which also contained some very distinctive pottery. Whatever provision they made for the living has left little trace in both cases. The other similarity is the pottery which was decorated with a herringbone pattern. Compare for yourself the pottery from Jericho and the pottery of the so-called 'Beaker Folk' in the book of that title by Harrison (see page 221).

The evidence suggests that it was a full two centuries before the West Semites started to use their energies to build on and settle in the Levant. For two centuries they returned to the nomadic ideal, at a time when I would think that there were few fixed boundaries, and such as there were were not as clear cut as now, but fluctuated continuously. Apart from the Wall of the Prince between Egypt and Asia, boundary stones were the chief means of fixing and marking such boundaries as there were.

In particular, in the hiatus at the end of the Early Bronze Age, there were huge migrating populations on the move like their nomadic ancestors, and the West Semites were one of them. Trying to imagine how far they would be likely to get in their wanderings on foot, I compared them with the last great foot-slog in history, Napoleon's catastrophic march to Moscow: Paris to Moscow in the spring and back to Paris in the (too) late autumn. But what if he had decided not to come back, but to go on? What if he had not lingered so long in Moscow? His troops could then have travelled three times the distance from Paris to Moscow in a single season, and I reckon they would have reached Peking. On foot. The world is very small even on foot.

But from this time there were also the great ocean-going vessels, which would have cut easier pathways round the globe, and made the world even smaller.

Yet the Hebrew chroniclers relate that Solomon's ships were away for three years. Where did they go? What did they bring back? We know very well where the Pharaohs of the New Empire got their wealth: the stupendous wealth of which we have some evidence in the Tomb of Tutankhamun. They did not have to go far for it, as they pillaged it all from their immediate neighbours, the West Semites. Amenophis II reports booty of 9,000 lbs of white gold in one expedition alone. Tuthmosis III similarly took vast quantities of gold. But where did the West Semites get it from? There were copper mines in Arabah, and turquoise mines in Sinai, but even for the tin they needed to make bronze, they would have had to go farther afield. Cornwall perhaps? Only last year it was reported for the first time that the copper mines of Wales were already being worked in 1500 BC, around the end of Solomon's empire. But there is no evidence as yet for similar ancient workings of the tin mines in Cornwall, but now that the possibility is there, people may begin to investigate it with a new eye.

Cornwall is named after the Cairns, or burial mounds, which are so striking. Which brings us to the names. Sometimes names get changed: from St. Petersburg to Leningrad, or from Eboracum to York, and sometimes they get changed back again later, as in the case of Byzantium. But often they just endure. And for this reason, in certain cases, they may provide clues back into prehistoric times about the early inhabitants, even the original inhabitants.

Evans-Wentz wrote a book on Celtic mythology, in which he comments on the possible connection between Carnac in Brittany and Karnak in Egypt. Cyrus Gordon has noted the omnipresence of the Dan people whose name crops up continuously in the Bronze Age. If Michael Astour and Danielou are correct, these would be the followers of the cult of Adonai, the Lord Osiris, who is reputed in Egyptian myth to have civilized the whole world.

But it is Philip Cohane, in *The Key*, who has carried out the most thorough investigation of ancient names. He devotes a chapter to the root BR, which he connects with EBER, ABRAM and the HEBREWS, and adds considerably to the evidence for finding them in the Americas, for example in the name BRAZIL. But he locates them notably in Italy as ABOR(i)genes (ABOR people), in IBERIA, BRITTANY and BRITAIN.

If they did colonize Britain, then it throws up an interesting possibility of a connection between King David and King Arthur. The acknowledged connections with Orpheus the fisher king, explored by Eisler, might then be pre-Christian and pre-Celtic and derive directly from the first imperial monarch in the Ancient Near East, King Keret, whom I identified with David in Part Two. Keret and Arthur are not unalike as names. David was surrounded by his 'mighty men', and presides over the twelve tribes which are related to the zodiac as we shall see. And Arthur had his twelve knights, and is associated with Glastonbury near the prehistoric zodiac thirty miles wide, cut into the hills, as described by Maltwood. There may even be some connection between Avaris and Avalon. In both stories the King's sickness is related to the barrenness of the land. This does not preclude the possibility of later British kings modelled on this ancient prototype, and adding new ingredients to the ancient legend. As Matthew Arnold put it, 'later authors of the tale are building with materials of an older architecture, greater cunning and more majestical'. But how much older is the question? But that is a minor point.

The main purpose of this section is to re-examine the possibility that our world culture was diffused from a single source in the Eastern Mediterranean. It gives an introduction to the myth itself, to indicate the paths by land and sea, along which it might have been carried across the world. The point is twofold.

First, the marked resemblance between the myths, originally demonstrated by Frazer, is not just because they all derive from the same archetypal core in the human psyche – the credibility of this theory has been stretched to breaking point.

Secondly, this myth is not the property of a small band of foreigners whose story could never have captivated us. On the contrary it is the story of the migrating herd of humanity itself, moving south (to India?) ahead of the last Ice Age and, in due course, returning to its old stamping grounds in the temperate north.

The hub of the story is the Ancient Near East, only because this is the crossroads of three continents, with an extraordinary mixture of inhabitants that acted like a catalyst, each upon the other: Europeans and Africans; Asians and Indians, as well as the curious Hurrians, whose language is yet again different to any of the other major groups.

Above all, the climate in the Ancient Near East has helped preserve some of the literature from the Age of Myth, whereas elsewhere it perished.

Only the silent stones remain as magnificent witnesses to the myth.

The Zodiac and the Heavens

The stones point to the stars.

The sophisticated work of Professor Thom and Keith Critchlow has demonstrated beyond reasonable doubt that the original purpose of the megalithic structures was accurate astronomical investigation. They were observatories for marking the seasons and fixing the calendar, as well as, perhaps, exploring the nature of time and the universe.

Which brings us back to Imhotep. Imhotep, whose story

has so much in common with the story of Joseph, built the first step pyramid which, like the megaliths, was orientated on the stars. And Imhotep was reputed to have devised the Egyptian calendar. In later classical times this calendar was still the most accurate known calendar and was adopted by the Romans and, eventually, by us.

It has been suggested that astronomy predates agriculture and navigation, as it is a necessary prerequisite for both. So Imhotep may have only introduced his calendar from elsewhere and, perhaps, revised it. I think this calendar became the common property of the whole ancient world in the Bronze Age, but only the Egyptian priesthood managed to transmit the essential features of it through the Dark Ages which followed.

In remote antiquity, as now, the most important features of the calendar are the Midwinter Solstice (21 December), the Spring Equinox (21 March), the Summer Solstice (21 June) and the Autumn Equinox (21 September). These are related to the four points of the compass and so provide our orientation in this universe and locate us in the time-space continuum, then as now.

The Great Pyramid was so orientated that at dawn of the Spring Equinox, for one day only, half of one face of the pyramid was cast in shadow as a result of a shallow dent in its surface.

Similarly, from the heelstones which he located, Critchlow has shown that the extraordinary structures on Bodmin Moor served to cover the rising sun, thereby protecting the naked eye, at dawn on particular festivals: Imbolc, forty days after the Midwinter Solstice (now Candlemas, 1 February); Beltane, forty days after the Spring Equinox (May Day, 1 May); and Samhain, forty days after the Autumn Equinox (now Halloween, 31 October). There was also a festival of Lugh (Lughassadh) forty days after the Summer Solstice (1 August).

More than the pyramids in Egypt, it is the obelisks which suggest the technology for building Stonehenge. Even in comparatively recent times, transporting and erecting these stones (to St. Peter's Square, Rome and the embankment of the Thames) presented major difficulties. They were described as petrified rays of the sun, which seems to suggest they originally marked particular important moments in the sun's journey. This was also the function, according to Champeaux, of the twin bronze pillars Jachin and Boaz, outside Solomon's Temple; and the massive Sea of Bronze may also have originally been part of the equipment for accurate observation of the night sky.

In Egypt all the great feasts and festivals started at nightfall. I would think that the Hebrew high places, with their wooden pillars connected with the Queen of Heaven (the Moon-goddess) were also similar observatories for night vigils. These high places were eventually condemned and torn down, but I doubt it was the original ancient astronomical wisdom that was condemned, but rather a corrupt and degenerate form of it, perhaps the beginnings of divination by means of personal horoscopes.

In what follows, when I talk about the ancient cult of the zodiac, I do not mean horoscopes. The men who had the vision and energy to build those great megalithic observatories and who could also build magnificent tombs for themselves, made scant provision for their daily lives, and don't appear to have been unduly concerned about their personal destiny in this life. Before the rise of ego-consciousness, which only later came to dominate and so limit men's thinking, it would be natural to be more involved in the corporate identity of mankind, and labour for generations not yet born; it would be natural to be more concerned with the universal and eternal destiny of mankind.

Just as the idea of prediction dogged and discredited the true understanding of dreams (until Freud rediscovered it), so horoscopes have dogged and belittled the true understanding of the zodiac since classical times.

The zodiac is the belt of stars along which the sun appears

to pass on a winding snakelike path between the Tropics of Cancer in the north and Capricorn in the south. It crosses the Equator at the Spring and Autumn Equinoxes. I think the Mesopotamians in remote antiquity knew all this starlore which took many centuries to recover after the Dark Ages. They speak of the Way of Enlil, later identified with Marduk and Assur, both figures of Osiris (whose name is Egyptian but a transliteration into glyphs of Azari, meaning Throne-of-the-Eye, one of the titles of Marduk). The month of July which, throughout the Semite world, was named after Osiris, follows the Midsummer Solstice, when the sun 'touches' the Tropic of Cancer. Then there was the Way of Anu, the central band of the whole sky, the Equator. And thirdly, there was the Way of Enki, the Goat-fish, called Enki by the Sumerians and Ea by the Semites, and known as Capricorn to this day; the Tropic of Capricorn, then as now?

In Egypt, the divine figure Aah or Iah had similar functions and characteristics to Ea. Ea was Lord of Wisdom and the Abyss, and Aah was the dark underworld form of the Moon-god, also associated with wisdom in Egypt. They would both seem to be associated with the moon at midwinter in the House of Capricorn. A similar dark form of Zeus in Greece was called Iowe. This is possibly the source of the Diovis of the Romans (Jove and Deus being the root forms of the words for 'Light' and 'Deity') who is related to Janus and his consort Jana (Diana), whose name is still honoured in the first month, January, the month of Capricorn. Sun and moon combine to measure time, passing through the twelve houses of the zodiac until they return to where they began, the beginning and end that encompasses the whole cycle: Pan the Goat-god, the All, the alpha and the omega of the year. I cannot help suspecting that this series of divine figures is related to the origins of the Hebrew God Iah, or Yahweh.

In remote antiquity there were several different New Years, of which the most important for the Semites in Mesopotamia was the Spring New Year when they celebrated creation all over again. And this would appear to be the New Year celebrated by the Semite priesthood of Memphis who were closely associated with Imhotep and, therefore, Joseph. Their god was Ptah, the Creator, who was incarnate in the form of the Apis Bull, which would be the first sign of the zodiac in the Age of Taurus, with the astrological New Year celebrated in the spring, then as now.

In his masterpiece, *From Fetish to God in Ancient Egypt*, Wallis Budge (1934, p.vi) has declared that the monotheistic theology of the priests of Memphis in the Pyramid Age is as spiritually profound as anything in Judaism or Christianity, and he compares one of the Egyptian texts with the Prologue of St. John's Gospel which has rightly been considered the last word, the ultimate proclamation, of Christian belief.

The theological system of the priests of Memphis as it existed under the Old Kingdom some five thousand years ago . . . arrived at the highest conception of God which was ever reached in Egypt, and their religion was a pure monotheism. They evolved the idea of God as a Spirit, a self-created, self-subsisting, eternal, almighty mind-god, the creator of all things, the source of all life and creation, who created everything that is merely by THINKING, HORUS being his heart or mind, and THOTH, the Word which gave expression to the thought which 'came into his mind'. Creation was the visible result of the utterances of his mouth. The other gods, e.g. those of Heliopolis, were only the *thoughts* of PTAH, the One God. As we work out the details of the text and the scheme of thought underlying them, it becomes clear that the Memphite theology can be fittingly described by the opening verses of the Gospel of St. John:

1. In the beginning was the Word, and the Word was with God and the Word was God.
2. The same was in the beginning with God.

3. All things were made by him; and without him was not any thing made that was made.
4. In him was life; and the life was the light of men.

If Joseph was Imhotep then this profound theology cannot but be associated with the early theology of the old Hebrews, because Imhotep was the most famous priest of Memphis. He was described later as the son of the God, Ptah. Like his Creator father, he was the master craftsman not only of the first step pyramid, close to Memphis, but also of the first temple of healing at Edfu, nearby. A thousand years later the foreign king Salitis (whom I identify with Saul) and the Semite kings ruled from there until they built their new capital at Avaris.

Budge himself has great difficulty reconciling the profound spirituality of the Ancient Egyptians with what he refers to as 'the rabble of gods' for which Ancient Egypt was notorious. He frequently mentions that the original nature of certain gods was 'stellar' because the vivid glyphs depict them with a star next to their names. Thus the original Divine Light takes particular forms and transformations in the course of time – the cycle of the year. This multitude of divine forms are the celestial beasts of the zodiac which could also have been incarnate on earth, because heaven and earth reflected each other.

The nine gods of Heliopolis, the City of the Sun, are described as the teeth of Ptah which mark the nine, or possibly eight, divisions of the older zodiac. Much of the apparent confusion of mythology, the amorphous nature of the gods, the way they swop attributes and change sex, could be due to the dynamic nature of the course of the sun and moon swinging through the zodiac. The sun at midwinter has very different characteristics to the sun in high summer. As just one example, Hercules the Sun-hero, being dressed in women's clothing could be explicable in terms of the sun in the sign of Virgo.

But the texts suggest that our ancestors in the Age of

Myth were quite aware that these were only images, but images of the underlying dynamics of life, the gods, and the life-force, God.

In an Akkadian text (possibly originating when Akkadian was the diplomatic language of Solomon's empire) it is stated: 'The stars are images or symbols ("tamshilu") of the gods.'

. And so the Heavens in all their manifold and changing appearances, became the image of Heaven, the dwelling-place of the power that generates and sustains the universe.

The Cycle of the Year and the Circle of the Gods

In their barrows in Britain some 4,000 years ago, the architects of the megalithic structures (the astronomer-priests?) were sometimes buried with their breastplates. Critchlow has deduced that these were accurate metal templates, like classroom protractors, but used for measuring particular angles rather than any angle. These templates would have been used for aligning the megaliths which, in turn, provided accurate markers of the detailed observation of the skies. He has also suggested a resemblance between these templates and the description of Aaron's breastplate which may have been used for aligning the stones below Mount Sinai, or arranging the circle of stones outside Jericho.

The precise angles of the metal plates were used, according to Critchlow, to site the megalithic structures on Bodmin Moor. The combined evidence of the templates and the megaliths suggests that the circle of the sky was divided into different portions: sacred angles that yield sacred numbers. In particular, he suggests a fivefold division, a sevenfold division and a ninefold division.

The angle of 72° yields the fivefold division of the circle. But this circle of 360° is divided to correspond with the 360 days of the year, plus five extra days, or six in a leap year. So, in terms of the calendar, this fivefold division yields five periods of seventy-two days.

Symbolically seventy-two is an interesting number. In the Age of Myth it crops up frequently. For example, Thoth played draughts with the moon (the measurer of time) and won from it one day in every seventy-two, so he won five days in all and used them to create five gods. In Egypt the calendar is 360 days but with five extra days outside the calendar that were traditionally the birthdays of Osiris, Isis, Seth, Nephtys and the infant Horus. But in this family there was a sixth figure: the bastard Anubis. Perhaps this figure once represented the 366th day of the leap year, but if so his significance was forgotten in the Dark Ages which followed the Age of Myth. But personally, I would be very surprised if so many accurate templates, megaliths, pyramids, obelisks, temples and other observatories had failed to calculate the leap year.

But that is only a detail. What really interests me is the possibility that these figures are associated with a five-part zodiac. Some people would prefer to limit the zodiac solely to the twelvefold division, but this is not in accord with its history, during which it has been divided up in many different ways, into unequal as well as equal parts. Osiris and Seth correspond to the archetypal brothers, Gemini. Isis is Virgo. Anubis who conducts the dead to the underworld and presides over the scales would seem to be associated with the Autumn Equinox and Libra, and Nephtys with midwinter, when the dead sun is restored, as she can restore the dead to life. And Horus with midsummer.

The most significant seventy-day period in remote antiquity was the absence of Adonis which lasted seventy days. And we still have a vestige of this division of the year into seventy-day periods in Septuagesima Sunday, once the seventieth day before Easter. When the minute observation is no longer carried out and the true significance of the number seventy-two gets forgotten it is easily rounded off to seventy.

With regard to the angle of 52°, it divides the circle of the sky and the cycle of the year into seven parts. Again in the fifty days from Easter to Pentecost, we may have a vestige of this sevenfold division of the year which appears to feature in the temple scroll from Qumran, and may underlie the sevenfold division of John's gospel: there are seven miracles possibly associated with seven festivals in the course of the year. In her book *The Older Testament*, Margaret Barker has suggested that the Christians were drawn originally from those Jews remaining loyal to an older (royalist) strand of their religion who had been ostracized by new reforms and taken refuge in Qumran and elsewhere. Far from being a late development, she sees the highly imaginative 'Apocalyptic' literature as a survivor from an earlier period – perhaps even from the Age of Myth?

Finally, there is Critchlow's ninefold division of the year which is perhaps the most significant of all in this context, because all the great companies of gods in Egypt were arranged in nines: at Memphis, Heliopolis, Khnum, and Thebes. At Memphis, Ptah was the first of the gods, with his company of eight. At Heliopolis Ra was the first with the same company of eight. The same eight gods were subject to Thoth at Khnum (the 'City of Eight') and Amon took precedence over the eight at Thebes. And I am inclined to think Jacob was originally the 'Father' of a similar (or the same) company of eight who were his legitimate offspring by his two wives Leah (meaning 'Cow') and Rachel (meaning 'Ewe'):

1 Taurus – Reuben, as firstborn of Leah (Cow) is the Bull. Son of Urru (Semite Sun-god, equivalent of Egyptian Ra.)
2 Gemini – Simeon and Levy, equivalent of the Semite Mot and Aleyin, and the Egyptian Seth and Osiris.
3 Leo – Judah, equivalent of the Egyptian Djehuti (Thoth). (Note: when only the tribe of Judah was

left, Iah-Djehuti, or Yahweh, may have been adopted as the one national god of the Jews.)

4 Virgo – Dinah, nearest equivalent of Diana of the Romans, consort of Janus. (Note: The Romans appear to have preserved traditions close to those of the Levant, possibly via the Etruscans – 'Tyrrhenians' from Tyre?).

5 Eagle-hawk (the older form of Scorpio) – Issachar, equivalent of the Egyptian Seker, the Hawk-god, whose consort was Selket, the Scorpion-goddess.

6 Sagittarius – Zebulun, equivalent of the Semite Baal Zebul, later nicknamed Baal Zebub, who was lord of flies and death. Sagittarius is death-dealing at the end of the sun's year.

7 Capricorn, the Water-god – Joseph, equivalent of Baal Saphon. The healing gods are associated with the healing of the sun's power after the Midwinter Solstice, but also with springs and water.

8 Pisces – Benjamin. Son of Yam, a Semite river god, possibly associated with Yama, Indian god of death, is the last sign before the spring New Year.

The year divided into nine parts gives nine periods of forty days. This forty-day period has remained significant in the Judaeo-Christian tradition, especially the forty days of Lent followed by the fifty days to Pentecost. Could it be that forty- and fifty-day periods always alternated in this way, and overlapped with the seventy-day periods as with Septuagesima and Lent? In any case, it seems all too likely that many such markers and divisions would be needed to assess and plot all the complex celestial phenomena.

The megalithic stones and the living tradition preserved from Egypt via the Hebrews both seem to point to the same divisions of the calendar, yielding specific pieces of information that will increasingly help us to reconstruct what was the obvious basis of religious life in remote antiquity and, indeed, still is: the calendar, the cycle of the year with its fasts and festivals.

But the difference in ancient times was that these various periods of the year were represented by divine figures with animal or semi-animal forms, which closely resemble the celestial beasts that have survived to this day as in the twelve signs of the zodiac. It seems strange to me that so little notice has been taken of attempts to relate the animal forms of the circle of the gods with the celestial beasts of the zodiac who divide the cycle of the year. The animal forms have mostly been taken in too earthy and literal a manner.

This starts with mistaking the mountain of the universe from which the Assembly of the Gods ruled for an actual mountain on earth. Even though it may be represented symbolically by an actual mountain (or pyramid), the Celestial Mountain is not of this world but has its apex at the Pole Star in the north, and its base is the circle of the zodiac. The ocean that surrounds the mountain is the vast ocean of outer space.

I do not deny that there were practical reasons for studying the stars, to do with navigation and agriculture. But these fail to reflect man's overwhelming passion in the Age of Myth, which was spiritual and scientific.

A New Assembly of Gods Rules Each New World Age

As soon as you start looking at the mythical animal forms of the gods in relation to the zodiac and time (the calendar), it yields some extraordinary results.

The name Ptah, equivalent of the Creator, is apparently close to a Hebrew word for 'opening', and is thought to be a Semite loanword appropriated by the Egyptians. And Ptah was incarnate in the Apis Bull which, in the Age of Taurus, would have opened the year. (Similarly, our word April is derived from the Latin 'Apero' to open.) This suggests that the Ptah-bull marked the Semite New Year at the Spring Equinox, and would have been associated with sunrise and the east.

By contrast, Seker meant 'to close'. As one of the four sons of Horus, the Hawk-god was also consort of the Scorpion-goddess, Selket. And the hawk (or eagle) is the old form of the sign of Scorpio, which stands directly opposite Taurus in the zodiac and would have been another of the four cardinal signs in the Age of Taurus. Ptah and Seker were sometimes combined as Ptah-seker. Ptah's consort was the lion-headed Sekhmet, associated with fire and the blazing heat of the sun. In the Age of Taurus, Leo was another cardinal sign marking the Midsummer Solstice. Finally, their son Nefertum is usually represented in human form as a man, with lotus in the waters, or a scimitar.

The bull, the lion, the hawk, and the man – does that remind you of anything? The same four celestial beasts which marked the four cardinal points in the Age of Taurus are the four forms of the beast in Ezekiel, and later represent the four Evangelists, Luke, Mark, John and Matthew. It may be significant that three of their feasts are still celebrated close to the Equinoxes and Winter Solstice - 25 April, 21 September and 27 December.

Now I want you to consider the picture on p.185. It is an illustration from the Egyptian *Book of the Dead*. Do the four large figures seem familiar? From the right, they are the Bull-god, the Lion-god, the Hawk-god and Khnum, the Goat-god, who is not only associated with Capricorn, but also with another Nile god, Hapi, who is sometimes represented as a man, with Urns, the Egyptian Aquarius.

In the same picture (third from the right on the top line), is a hare. This excited me when I first noticed it, because although the hare does not feature in the Western zodiac as we know it, it does feature the Far Eastern zodiac. The hare was the great mother-goddess

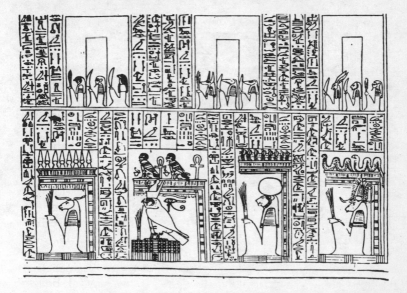

Fig.6   Illustration from the Egyptian Book of the Dead.

in Ancient Egypt (with her cult at Hermopolis) and was held to be a form of the Sun-god, Ra and the Moon-god, Osiris: in terms of the zodiac these divine figures would have taken the form of the hare when in that sign of the zodiac.

But the hare is also associated with the very ancient Titan-goddess, Hecate, in Greece. Hecate was known as three-formed, and her three forms were the lion, the horse and the dog. (See page 186.) But apart from the lion (equivalent of the eastern tiger) these forms do not feature in the Western zodiac, but do in the Far Eastern zodiac. What is more, they each come four months apart, so divide the year into the three equal parts, which is consistent with Egypt's three-season year.

Hecate is normally numbered among the Titans: the twelve old gods who were overthrown and replaced. This

185

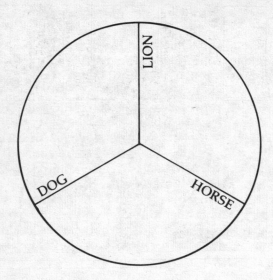

Fig. 7   Hecate's three forms in relation to the Far Eastern Zodiac.

is a feature of many myths, and it is usually twelve who
have to go, to make room for a new assembly of twelve; in
this case, Zeus and the twelve gods of Mount Olympus.

Similarly, in Mesopotamia, Tiamat and her eleven demons
had been overthrown by the god of the East Semites
(Marduk). Among these twelve ancient demons are familiar
forms from our zodiac: the destructive spirits of anger
(Gemini?), the Great Lion, the Scorpion-man, and the
Fish-ram. But other forms feature in the Far Eastern zodiac
only: the Serpent, the Gruesome-hound and the Dragon (a
nine-headed creature like the Greek Hydra).

But Hydra, like the gruesome Cerberus-dog, and the
Nemean lion, was also an offspring of the Titans. It was the
task of the Sun-hero, Hercules, to subdue these creatures,
as well as other animal forms familiar to us from the zodiacs
of East and West, for example, the Cretan bull, the girdle of

the Amazon (Virgo?), the eagle, the mares, the hind and the boar.

Again in Rome, Janus had been the first of the old assembly of gods, and continued to be revered himself as the first among gods – but it was Jupiter who ruled the new assembly.

I don't want to get too bogged down with details, but if the astronomer priests did their job properly then it isn't just the first sign that needs to be changed with each new world age but all the signs would have to be adapted to the new celestial situation in each successive age: the Age of Gemini (6th–4th Millennium BC); the Age of Taurus (4th–2nd Millennium BC); the Age of Aries (2nd–0 Millennium BC); the Age of Pisces (0–2nd Millennium AD) and again now as we move into the Age of Aquarius. Whether this is done or not seems to depend on the vitality of the cult. It would appear that it has not been done in the West since the Age of Aries (2000 BC). But apart from changing the first signs (the bull, the rat and the pig) in successive world ages, the Far Eastern zodiac appears to derive from the Age of Gemini (6000–4000 BC).

That is to say, if you speculate that the Far Eastern zodiac became fixed after the Age of Gemini, while the Western wheel of life moved on twice and only became fixed with Aries as the first sign, then if you move our zodiac back two places, it corresponds much more closely with the Eastern zodiac, as you will see on page 188.

But this Eastern zodiac also appears to have been the old zodiac of Egypt, Mesopotamia, Greece and Rome, and many of the myths of those places appear explicable in terms of it. Also, the Hebrew zodiac shows vestiges of it.

For example, another illustration from the *Egyptian Book of the Dead* appears to contain almost exactly these twelve figures from the Eastern zodiac, and throws light on them and their connection with the later Western zodiac. (See Fig. 9, page 189.)

In it, the corpse is flanked by Isis and Nephtys and the

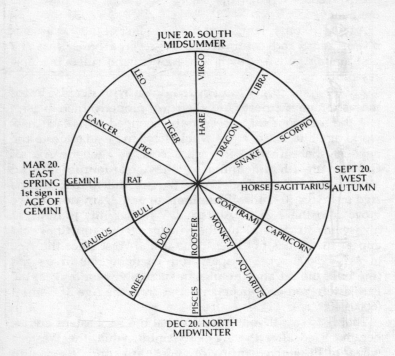

Fig. 8   The Far Eastern Zodiac in relation to the Western Zodiac in the Age of Gemini

four sons of Horus, which are variants of the four cardinal signs of the zodiac. In particular, the jackal (surely the equivalent of the Eastern rat) is called the 'Opener of the Ways', suggesting a time when he opened the year. The jackal is also a form of Seth, the archetypal twin, so Gemini. Many of the myths seem to have twins as their starting point (Shu and Tefnut in Egypt, Jacob and Esau in the Hebrew account) and dual figures like Janus, almost a Siamese twin.

188

Fig.9   Illustration from the Egyptian Book of the Dead.

A Note on the Sumerians: Their Origin and Their Fate

If there is a connection between the Far Eastern zodiac and an Ancient Egyptian zodiac, then how can we account for it? The only identifiable and plausible connection between Egypt and the Far East is the Sumerians, who were a powerful influence at the roots of civilization in both Mesopotamia and Egypt.

Recent studies have been finding more and more in common between the roots of Hindu and Hebrew religion, for example the Indian 'chakras' of yoga on Sumerian cylinder seals, a tentative identification of Abraham and Sara with Brahma and Sara-vastri, and much else. Doane in the last century had already drawn up many parallels. And Danielou identifies Osiris with Shiva (as well as Dionysos), and suggests that the Sumerians are related linguistically to the Tamil-speaking Indians who may well have lived further north (in the Indus Valley?) before being pushed south by the conquering Celtic-Vedic people.

So far, there is no material evidence of high civilization in India before the rise of the Sumerian-Semite culture on the Euphrates, and the Sumerian-Hamite culture on the Nile. So the question arises: how could the Sumerians have brought civilization to these places if they didn't already have it to bring?

As there isn't much evidence I can only guess (and your guess may be better than mine). I think that then, as now, the Indians had a more highly evolved spiritual life, and what they brought with them when they came to the Ancient Near East was a vital spiritual ingredient which acted like a catalyst on the more materialistic Semites and Hamites. And I think this continued to be their vital contribution throughout The Age of Myth.

There is no evidence that the Sumerians were ever exterminated. Sargon of Agade allowed them to remain strong enough to found another dynasty after his. But meanwhile there is evidence that they were also moving north and west into Assyria and Syria. The Assyrians claimed to be the continuity of Sumer and Agade, and continued to use the Sumerian language for ritual purposes, which suggests a Sumerian priesthood. And the library at Ebla in Syria contains texts in Sumerian as well as archaic Hebrew. The empire of Old Assyria reached across much of Syria and Israel, as far as Tyre at one time. I wonder if there isn't a connection between Sumer and Samaria, as well as between Tyre and Tyrrheneans (Etruscans) who spoke an agglutinative language similar to Sumerian.

Interestingly, Aristotle thought the Hebrews were Indian, as quoted by Josephus who does not deny it. Samaria was famous for its ivories, which suggests a continuing Indian connection, since the elephant was long extinct in the Near East. Tuthmosis III hunted them on the Euphrates, but it is thought there was just a small reserve of them by then.

The Hebrew Connection

If you accept the Bronze Age as a period of international contacts and worldwide colonization, then the mythology arising out of the cycle of the zodiac tends to confirm and corroborate the event from a completely different angle. The worldwide spread of the zodiac tends to suggest the purpose behind the worldwide presence of megalithic structures which were aligned to the stars. The ability to adjust the zodiac to each new age is in accord with the detailed knowledge of the stars which Thom and Critchlow have detected in the stones. The precision of the Egyptian calendar matches the precision of the alignments.

The specific focus of my studies has been at the crossroads of all this activity: the West Semites and the Old Phoenicians, with their great ports along the eastern shores (and offshore islands) of the Mediterranean. The Greeks themselves always acknowledged their debt to the Phoenicians as an important source of their civilization and culture which was brought to them by either Cadmus or Danaeus, brother of Egyptus and ancestor of the Danoi. Recent studies (such as the work of M. Astour) are showing this debt to be increasingly large.

The particular contribution of this survey is to identify the Hebrews with those same West Semites and Old Phoenicians in the Bronze Age. But if this is so, the Hebrews were priests of On and Memphis, and they brought out of Egypt the religion of Egypt. The whole study would make no sense if it cannot be shown that the Hebrews, like the Egyptians and the West Semites, subscribed to the old religion that was universally accepted and was based on the zodiac. It has to be via them, at the crossroads, that the culture of Mesopotamia and Egypt reached Greece,

Crete, Rome and the rest of the ancient world. Leonard Woolley and Theodore Gaster (in very different ways) have thrown a lot of light on this pathway of civilization, and its dissemination.

In connection with this universal myth, the most important evidence is the relationship between the twelve signs of the zodiac and the twelve Hebrew tribes. With regard to the specific identification of each tribe with a particular sign, there is a long tradition of muddle going back into classical times. By then, the Bronze Age society had been fragmented and its myth shattered and, most especially, the whole concept of the different world ages had been lost. In other words, it was the failure to distinguish between the old zodiacs that has led to the confusion. For vestiges of the old zodiac linger on in the New Age, as we saw with the bull, lion, hawk and man.

So I want first to look at the world ages again, firstly in India where the evidence seems most clearly related to the zodiac. There, through ten world ages, the god Vishnu was reincarnated ten times in the form of fish, turtle (a variant form of Cancer), wild boar and lion – forms with which we are familiar through the zodiac.

Similarly, in Berosus's chronicle of Mesopotamian history, there were ten kings before the Flood who reigned for a total of 432,000 years. These figures are plainly astronomical (they add up to a total of eighteen full cycles of twelve world ages, rounded off at 2,000 years each instead of the more precise 2,160). The Hebrew chroniclers also record ten generations before the Flood, but the accumulated lifespans of these figures add up to a more modest 8,000 years or four world ages.

For astronomers, all the former world ages that lie behind the present one can be worked out theoretically. But as far as I can discern from the myths themselves, the true beginning of the zodiac was in the Age of Gemini. For me, some of the clearest indications of this come from the Bible. Bearing in mind that the different ages have been referred to in history as 'generations', Jacob the father of the twelve tribes, is the twin brother of Esau: 'Behold, there were twins in her womb. The first came forth red, all his body like a hairy mantle; so they called him Esau' (*Genesis* 25. 24–26). Afterwards his brother came forth, and his hand had taken hold of Esau's heel, so his name was called Jacob. Even to this day the Gemini twins are usually depicted as being joined by a cord or touching. The hairy redness is reminiscent of the rays of the rising and setting sun in the east and the west, and the Spring and Autumn Equinoxes. In the next generation, Reuben, as firstborn of Leah, meaning 'Cow', is probably Taurus. Reuben slept with his father's concubines, which is another way of saying that he took his father's place. But in the end, he who was once 'pre-eminent' also had his day, and was replaced by Joseph, firstborn of Rachel, meaning 'Ewe', hence Aries, as was foretold in Joseph's dream: 'Behold, the sun, the moon, and eleven stars were bowing down to me.' His star, Aries, came to take precedence over that of Taurus and of Gemini. This transition from the Age of Taurus to the Age of Aries took place at the end of the Pyramid Age, which was also the time when Moses condemned the cult of the golden calf (Taurus?).

In Egypt the transition appears to have been taken very seriously and caused an enormous upheaval. In the Age of the Bull, the pharaohs of the old kingdom were crowned at Memphis which was their capital, and the centre of the cult of the Apis Bull, incarnation of Ptah. At the beginning of the Age of Aries, the capital was moved to Thebes, an insignificant village until then, where the cult centred on the Ram-god, Amon, and several pharaohs adopted the name Amenemhet, meaning 'Amon leads'.

In India (Harappa in the Indus Valley) a zodiac has been found which appears to date from the beginning of the Age of Aries, and is closely related to our present Western zodiac, the new zodiac, although it has only eight signs. They are: the ram (Aries); the harp (instrument of Apollo, twin of Artemis – so Gemini); the crab (Cancer); the mother

(Virgo); the scales (Libra); the pitcher (Aquarius), and the fish (Pisces). Interestingly, the missing signs are the bull, lion, hawk (Scorpio) and goat, the four cardinal signs of the previous age.

I think I have said enough to make it clear that when we come to assign the twelve tribes to the twelve houses of the zodiac, we are juggling with eight and twelve signs in three world ages. So we must be a little flexible in our approach to match the fluidity of the zodiac with all its shifts and changes, some of which derive from a thousand years before the beginning of the Age of Myth: the Age of Gemini.

Before attempting to assign houses to the tribes, I would like to introduce the Blessings of Jacob (*Genesis*, Chapter 49) and Moses (*Deuteronomy*, Chapter 33), which are the main cause for the fairly widespread agreement that the tribes were once related to the zodiac. These chapters are in especially archaic Hebrew, suggesting that they are some of the oldest sections in the Bible as we know it, and in a learned article, B. Vawter discerned references to the old West Semite pantheon of gods as described in the literature from Ugarit.

In these Blessings, the sons of Jacob (like the tribes descended from them) bear a striking resemblance to the signs of the zodiac, as if they were the earthly counterparts of the constellations. And we know that like the revolving zodiac, the tribes served a central shrine by monthly rota (as was also the custom in Sumeria and at Delphi).

Here are the more obvious references to the zodiac from the two chapters:

Taurus: 'The firstling bull has majesty and his horns are the horns of the wild ox.'

Gemini: 'The brothers will be divided for their anger is fierce.'

Cancer (pig in the old zodiac): Nothing.

Leo: 'As a lion, and as a lioness . . . Like a lion he tears the arm . . . a lion's whelp that leaps forth.'

Virgo: "The blessings of the breasts of the womb.'

Libra (scales of justice): 'He shall judge his people.'

Scorpio (snake in the old zodiac): 'A serpent in the way, a viper by the path, that bites the horse's heels.' (And the next sign is the horse.)

Sagittarius (ass in the old zodiac, then horse): 'A strong ass.' And possibly 'Raiders shall raid, but he shall raid on their heels.'

Capricorn: 'A hind let loose.'

Aquarius: 'A bough by a spring . . . the blessings of the deep beneath.'

Pisces (dog in the old zodiac, not differentiated from wolf – Anubis was dog-headed or wolf-headed): 'A ravenous wolf devouring the prey.'

Aries: Possibly the 'sheepfolds' and the 'shepherd'.

At this distance in time it may not be possible to restore the Hebrew zodiac in its entirety for three reasons: first, the three different world ages (Gemini, Taurus and Aries) involved a reshuffle of the zodiac each time; secondly, the Bible is drawn from Northern, Southern and Eastern traditions, and as we know from Egypt, different companies of gods ruled in different areas; and thirdly, because of the reforms which expressly forbade the cult of the stars in the time of Hezekiah, Josiah and Jeremiah, when the Bible was being heavily revised.

Nevertheless, where the order of the tribes at their birth (*Genesis* 29/31ff), or in the Blessings, coincides with the order of celestial beasts in the zodiac, this would suggest a reliable base to start from as follows on page 196.

1	Aries	–	
2	Taurus	–	
3	Gemini	'Brothers'	Simeon and Levy
4	Cancer	–	
5	Leo	'Lion'	Judah
6	Virgo	–	
7	Libra	'Judge'	Dan
8	Scorpio (old serpent)	'Serpent'	(also Dan)
9	Sagittarius	'Raider'	Gad
10	Capricorn	'Hind'	Naphtali
11	Aquarius	'Spring'	Joseph
12	Pisces (old dog)	'Wolf'	Benjamin

Of the missing signs, some can be filled in with more certainty than others. As the firstborn, and coming before the 'Brothers', Reuben would seem to be Taurus: like Taurus he loses his pre-eminence at the end of the Age of Taurus, and is replaced by Joseph-Ephraim, described as 'prince among his brothers' and the new 'firstling'. To Cancer I have assigned Asher, although there are no strong reasons for it (see, however, Cancer, below). However, there appears to be no difficulty in assigning Virgo, the only feminine sign, to Dinah, the only sister among the twelve. In some old zodiacs, Scorpio was a double-sign, and the claws of the Scorpion formed Libra the scales of justice, as above. None the less, I think Issachar, because of the Egyptian

Seker-Selket connection, was also associated with Scorpio. And possibly Zebulun (next in order of birth) with Sagittarius. Capricorn the goat-fish was also the healing god of the Deep Water Abyss, Enki, in Mesopotamia, Khnum in Egypt and Eshmun in Sidon – so Naphtali the 'Hind' may be related in this way to Neptune, Lord of Sidon, i.e. Po-seidon.

1 **Aries** *Joseph-Ephraim* Ephraim was Joseph's younger son who, like Joseph before him, was destined to become pre-eminent over his older brother. Strictly speaking, from the old zodiac the Age of the Bull should have been followed by the Age of the Dog – but this is where the adjustment of the whole zodiac to the new age comes in. In remote antiquity the dog does not appear qualified to take the first position. So it is the next sign in the old eight-part zodiac which bifurcates into the Goat-god (Khnum in Egypt) with long wavy horns and the Ram-god (Amon) with spiralling horns (for the spring). In the same way Joseph (the Capricorn-Aquarius figure of the old zodiac) bifurcates in his two sons Manasseh and Ephraim. Though changed from bull to ram, this is still the month of the 'opening' of the year, and so sacred to the Creator Gods, Egyptian Ptah, (or Phtah) and West Semite Kothar. The Greek God Priapus was patron of shepherds, had spiralling horns and phallic creativity.

2 **Taurus** *Reuben* Along with other reasons already mentioned for identifying Reuben with Taurus, the fact that he is the firstborn of the twelve sons places the story firmly in the Age of Taurus. He would appear to be the son of Ra (sometimes Re) in Egypt and the West Semite Urru.

3 **Gemini** *Simeon* and *Levi* Possibly the month sacred to Mot and Aleyin, the West Semite deities known from Ugarit.

4 **Cancer** *Asher* Assur was one of the Semite names

for Adonis-Osiris. Another was Tammuz, and Cancer (June–July) was the month of Tammuz. The 'Wailing for Osiris' took place in this month when Sirius was absent from the night sky. According to some accounts he was killed by a wild pig (the old form of Cancer) and his testicles were eaten by a crab, which may have an astrological significance.

5 **Leo** *Judah* The Blessings associate Judah with the lion: 'Judah . . . couched as a lion.' And the lion of Judah became proverbial. This month (July–August) was the Egyptian month of Djehuti, meaning 'He of Djehut', (the unnamed god – called Thoth by the Greeks). In the Bible a man of Judah is referred to as 'Jehudi'.

6 **Virgo** *Dinah* In an Elephantine text, the consort of Iah was the West Semite goddess Anat, who may have been historicized in the Bible as Nathan. And in Rome, the consort of Janus was Diana.

7 **Libra** *Dan* As the scales suggest, this month, following the Autumn Equinox, has long been associated with the Judgement of the Dead. The Blessings once more appropriately suggest that 'Dan shall judge his people'. Dan is an abbreviation of Adonis, the Lord, namely Osiris who was Judge of the Dead in Egypt. His West Semite name was Hay-Tau (another possible source of the name Yah-Veh).

8 **Scorpio** *Issachar* Like Seker in Egypt, Issachar marked the 'close' of the year in autumn in the Age of Taurus, in the form of a hawk/eagle. When moved down into the underworld in the Age of Aries, this form would no longer be appropriate, so it was likely to have been for this reason that it was changed to Scorpio. In the Blessings, Issachar is 'a strong ass' which may be an association surviving from the Age of Gemini when it was the sign of the Ass which would have marked the close of the year, opposite Gemini. We have traces of Issachar changing role through the three world ages

of Gemini, Taurus and Aries, as Ass, Eagle/Hawk and finally Scorpio.

9 **Sagittarius** *Zebulun* (and possibly Gad) The humble ass is now equipped with weapons, as the centaur – suited to the bull-rounding and bull-slaying ceremonies of the lesser Dionysia, in December. The Greater Dionysia continued to be held in March (when tragedies were performed). Could this be a vestige from the Age of Gemini when the sign of Taurus fell in March? Bachos the 'Roarer' was a title of Osiris and Dionysos, as well as Bacchus in Rome.

10 **Capricorn** *Naphtali* 'Naphtali is a hind let loose' in the Blessings. And December–January is the month of Poseidon in the Greek calendar. Po-Seidon stands for the Baal of Sidon, a Phoenician deity, equivalent of the Roman Neptune.

11 **Aquarius** *Joseph–Manasseh* Healing is associated with the Midwinter Solstice when the sun begins to regain its strength, and Eshmun was the West Semite lord of healing who, like Imhotep, was identified with the Greek Asklepios.

12 **Pisces** *Benjamin* The fierce Ben-Yammin (Sons of Yam) are known from the Bronze Age. Yam was a Semite river-god. In the Blessings, Benjamin is the devouring wolf which seems to be derived from the old zodiac. There may be a connection with Yama the Indian god of Death – in which case he remains appropriately stationed at the end of the cycle of the year, as in the older eight-part zodiac.

These twelve divisions of the zodiac were (and still are) further subdivided, much as our months are divided into weeks and days. Each sign was divided into three parts, giving thirty-six ten-day periods ('decans'). These played an especially prominent part in Egypt, and the number of their provinces probably reflected this division of the zodiac just as the Hebrew tribal states reflected the twelve-part division. But these thirty-six could be further subdivided into seventy-two five-day periods, each with a celestial beast or divine figure to represent it – hence the 'rabble of gods' which Budge so deplored. But set back in their context of the zodiac, it becomes obvious that these are only temporary forms, manifestations or powers of the one divine essence described in Budge's text from Memphis.

In the Pyramid Age, the priesthood of Memphis does not appear to have had any difficulty in accommodating the one lord with the many forms. The first piece of evidence we have of an attempt to exclude the many is the short text already quoted about Apophis-Solomon who would not worship any god but Sutekh in the sixteenth century BC. Then there were the more renowned reforms of Akhenaten shortly after, in the fourteenth century BC. But the tombs at Jericho provide one other clue: Kathleen Kenyon describes them as very similar to Egyptian tombs of the same period, except that there were no images of any gods. This suggests that the Hebrews already had a more psychological view of the forms.

Within the framework of the zodiac, the forms and transformations of the gods were precious and illuminating, reflecting the changes and transformations of life and nature. But robbed of the accurate astronomy that underpinned the old religion, the myths became obscure and faintly ridiculous. So the established religions all over the world increasingly threw in their lot with the one essential point, the divine essence, to the exclusion of the many forms.

The many forms did linger on, however, and in many forms, particularly in the Apocalyptic writing, first Jewish then Christian, with its orders of angels that must outnumber the gods of Egypt. They also feature in such traditions as the emanations of divine powers of the Gnostics, the sephiroth of the Kabala (those blazing spheres of conscious energy that emanate from heaven to earth, and so mediate between

God and man), and the curious divine-demonic forces that helped the work of alchemy which allegedly came from Egypt (Kem, the black land, being the old name for Egypt).

Although you can see how the saints and angels have filled the cycle of the Christian year, very much as the divine forms had in the old religion, nevertheless there was an obvious split. It reflects the split in the human mind between intellect and imagination. God became increasingly an intellectual abstraction, very far from the fleshy Sacred Bull, which was black, white or piebald depending on which of the heavenly figures it was to represent.

Meanwhile, the heavenly figures, robbed of their intellectual content came increasingly to seem like vague mystification. Both sides had been impoverished by the split, which also reflects the split between thinking and feeling, between analysis and creativity, but above all between conscious and unconscious. Comparatively small groups like the Romantics in the last century, and now the Jungians, struggle with the dark, unconscious content of the mind, little helped by the main body of society. So one hemisphere of the brain atrophies or putrefies, unseen.

Perhaps, once it is fully appreciated that both traditions derive from a single source in the Pyramid Age when mankind achieved a youthful flowering of all his capacities, then each side of the great divide could learn to cherish the other, and thereby enrich their own standpoint, or worldview. Perhaps. At least, that is what I hope. Like the ancient priests of Memphis.

A Note on Imhotep-Joseph, in Cult

In the Age of Aries, Nefertum with his scimitar was replaced by Imhotep with his healing staff and serpent. Whereas the son of Ptah and Sekmet was in the death-dealing position of Sagittarius in the Age of Taurus, he is moved on in the Age of Aries to Capricorn's position; the time when the sun regains its strength, the time of healing, therefore Nefertum, the killer,

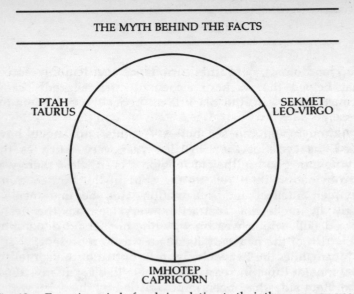

Fig. 10   Egyptian triad of gods in relation to their three-season year.

is replaced by the more appropriate Imhotep, the healer. This is illustrated on page 202. But this is the position which we have assigned to Joseph, for quite other reasons, in the older eight-part zodiac, and to Joseph–Manasseh in the twelve-part Hebrew zodiac. Which suggests it wasn't just the life of the two figures which had points in common, but also the later cult.

A Note on Place Names, Personal Names and the Gods

It is generally acknowledged that the names of the Hebrew tribes may have been derived originally from ancient deities, though these are hardly ever specified except in the case of Issachar and Seker. In the same way there is a volume of erudite work on the subject of Hebrew place names and personal names which often honour ancient Semite deities, although in some cases there has been an attempt to disguise this fact. Two examples are Jerusalem, which combines the divine figure of Urru (a sun-god) and Salem (dusk), and Samson, which honours Shamash (another Semite sun-god). Helmer Ringgren delves into this subject in some detail.

The Universal Mandala of Time and the Psyche

A mandala is a still picture of the forces at work in the universe, like a wind chart. It is a static pattern used to depict a dynamic sequence, like a map with arrows and dotted lines used to make a journey – in this case the journey of life. The Tibetans make their mandalas out of brightly coloured powders which are blown away soon after the pictures are completed. This helps keep the pictures close to what they are trying to depict: the continuously changing patterns of life. They picture the forces at work at the present moment, which is the culmination of the past and the seed of the future. The picture is valid for a moment, then everything changes as the picture is dissolved to make room for a new one.

The zodiac is like the vast prototype of all such pictures: it is the ever changing pattern of sun, planets and stars that governs the changes between day and night, summer and winter, youth and age, and synchronizes the present moment with the succession of world ages. This heavenly chart is a picture of the forces at play in the universe, as well as a significant image of man's life.

Time and life are interwoven like an intricate web with threads spun in many directions, and the zodiac provides an image of life in its context: time. Time, though vitally important, is invisible whilst the forces which rule life are intangible. So, without some such picture, the very dynamics of life are inclined to be elusive and to fade from view. The sun's journey from dawn to dusk and from spring to winter is the image of life's journey from birth to death. It also depicts the cycle of transformation and renewal that affects all nature.

This is the context of myth. This is the overall framework in which particular symbols and episodes from myth find their place.

The universal story is man's story. The sun's journey is also man's journey. The movements in the heavens reflect the movements on earth. One throws light on the other. The rising of the constellation Taurus was related to the rutting in the spring, and both were used in the myths to throw light on human life and human behaviour, arising out of human psychology. The myths themselves made this plain: the Celestial Bull, Taurus, was reflected in nature as the actual bull selected to be the sacred bull, which was mummified when it died; but there was also the bull-man in between as it were, which indicates that the myth was also about man and his psychology.

The sun-god who journeys in a boat or drives a chariot across the oceans of space is depicted as a human figure in the celestial setting. On earth, men also voyage across the earth's oceans and drive chariots along its highways. And somewhere between these two is the legendary sun-hero, setting sail. All three are different valid ways of telling the same story, altered perhaps to suit the taste of the audience. I suspect that Jason with his fifty argonauts, was none other than Janus, or the sun at the outset of its journey. With each new adventure one of the argonauts was snatched away, as the weeks, too, are snatched away. The prize was the Golden Fleece, and this fleece was a variant form of Aries the ram, which suggests the precious discovery of the cycle of eternal renewal.

The zodiac is the rim of the vast cauldron of renewal, which features in many myths and stories as a vessel of various kinds, notably the Grail, with its twelve guardian knights. This vessel is studded with many jewels from myth; far too many to count and number here. The Age of Myth alone lasted 2,500 years, but it also preserved and reset treasures from earlier ages . . . both consciously in its myth, ritual and drama and unconsciously. Long periods of evolution have left their mark on the way the body is formed, but they have also left their trace in the mind, particularly the unconscious, which is the end product of a very long process.

Dreams, symbols and myth are the natural language of

the unconscious, the language it uses even when we are asleep. But this is also the language of the creative imagination which can provide images of the deepest feelings and profoundest intuitions concerning the nature of time and life, and produce the changes and transformations of life that leave their trace in the psyche which, in turn, affect the next phase of life. Jungian psychology has drawn on the insights of East and West, from remote antiquity to the present day to throw light on these changes.

Each society has found its own images. Just one example is the Chinese *Book of Changes*, which is closely structured according to the seasons of the year. Its trigrams mark the seasons. It describes the workings of human life in terms of the workings of the universe, and asks to be read not from cover to cover, but in a variable way that is in deep accord with the variations of life. Like the zodiac it derives from the Age of Myth, and uses its own particular imagery to refer to the same human lifespan and destiny. It takes the line as its image of the core of life and uses it, broken and unbroken, to form patterns which display the changing forms life takes.

In the West, the images have gone a different way, taken a different shape. But the essential points remain the same. The images are different but they are still images of the core of life and the way it manifests in the forces at play in the universe and the psyche.

The language of images, the language of the unconscious, is a spontaneous, universal language. Nevertheless it still needs to be understood; this is part of the process of the psyche coming to grasp its own nature.

Images are a veritable riot of forms, the 'rabble of gods' which Budge so deplored. But as they are a part of us which cannot be removed, they need a shape, a context which is in accord with the shape and context of life. This cannot be imposed arbitrarily. The natural structure needs to be discovered and rediscovered to give shape to the myth. In the Age of Myth this shape was provided by the cycle of the year and the circle of divine figures who ruled it.

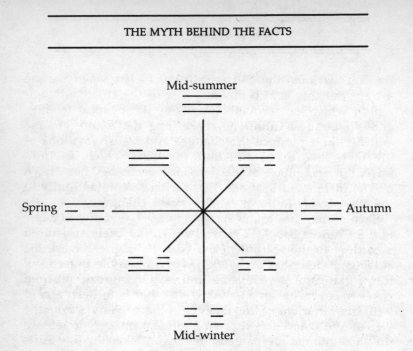

Fig. 11   Eight three-line patterns are like an eight-part sacred calendar, corresponding to the cycle of the year.

And this myth served to transform the pointless treadmill of existence into a meaningful cycle of life. So the riot of forms are given a sequence and a value.

Jung suggested that the night sky was a suitable vessel for all the images which the soul projects. In particular, the wheeling zodiac seems a large enough vehicle to accommodate all the forms which man can devise. It encompasses the vast, yet registers the moment. It could contain the myriad different symbols and myths without having to violate the specific nature of each.

If the zodiac was at the root of the major world religions in the Bronze Age, then this could relate the current 'rabble' of divergent images and forms which have emerged and continue to emerge in the succession of world ages.

206

The New Myth Grounded in the Old

The living book of the soul is already indelibly inscribed. Nothing can be changed of what has been, or of the trace it has left. The soul is experienced inwardly, deeply, and often turbulently. Its language is ancient, and therefore often archaic and difficult; it is the language of dreams and imagination. It can be frightening to battle alone with the soul, but it is worse to lose sight of it altogether. The soul is very particular and very personal, the end product of a particular line. But in its depths, this special personal soul is linked to the universal fabric of the human soul; it is like a particular fruit which is the product of one family tree, but also of the universal tree of life. The chains of DNA are the equivalent of this tree of life, and scientists believe they point back to a single womb for the whole human race. Interestingly, the double-spiral form of DNA also features in the twisting tendrils of the Tree of Life in many a stained glass window and illuminated manuscript.

What is experienced most personally and felt in the most intense and private way, has roots in common with all intense subjective experience. Our most private feelings are also plain feelings – love and hate. Our flashes of intuition that bring with them the most personal insights can be further illuminated by the insights of others, even though they lived in remote antiquity, or the Far East. Even our particular illusions and lunacies share the nature of lunacy and illusion in general. This is the deeply inward world of living experience, of which we barely scratch the surface.

So we come to the idea that this inward living experience is a proper object of study; perhaps the most necessary and valuable object of study for man. It could make all the difference between reasonable and irrational people, or between sane and mad behaviour. This is the difficult work of the science of the inward man, the science of the soul: psychology. Particularly difficult because the soul is invisible and intangible, and manifests only in images: images from dreams; images from works of imagination, and images from myth.

We need a myth if we are to throw light on the experience of the soul, in the way we human beings experience the life of the universe, which is both in us and all around us at the same time. The Zen teachers have often repeated, there is no inside and no outside. The more deeply you look inwards, the more you find there the same content as the content of the universe. What would the psyche be if it had been isolated in a total vacuum from the beginning? It is experience that has left its mark and trace in the living tissue. It is the dynamic universe in all its transformations through time, not just the static universe of space at one moment only.

No wonder Jung found the universe a suitable vessel for the soul of man. Its rim is the zodiac of stars. We orientate ourselves within it by the four cardinal points. We watch and experience the transformations of the seasons and the coming and going of lives, as the wheel of life turns.

The soul is our time-machine. We have taken a trip to ancient Egypt and back again. We can dip in where we like. Everything in the universe is accessible, open to being part of our very own experience. We reflect each other, the universe and I. We deserve each other. Life and matter, we both contribute to the end product: the stream of living experience. This is the dance of life and we, too, can learn to juggle with the spheres.

The modern era has been an age of division; an age of the emerging conscious ego, and part of the nature of egoism is to divide. There are collective egos as well as personal egos, whose nature is also to stand alone: nation against nation; religion against religion.

The ego is a great prize, the very fire stolen from the gods, the forbidden fruit of the Tree of Life, plucked away by each one of us. In the universe, the image of the ego is the sun itself. But in its mythic journey the sun must sink into the Western sea each night, and for longer and longer periods towards midwinter when the rays of the sun's strength are shorn. It dies and dissolves back into the night. Its light is shattered into millions of fragments – the stars – until it is restored and rises again. The ego, and collective egos, can be refreshed in the same way. This can be induced, but it also happens in the course of nature, in the course of time.

It happened dramatically and tragically at the end of the Bronze Age when a society was fragmented and their myth shattered. Different small fragments were preserved in various ways and in scattered places. But I think the real trace of the old myth has remained in the soul of man.

An exterior reflection of that trace was preserved in the Bible, a partial image only, treasured by the few survivors of the race that had once disseminated the myth. They had fragments, bits and pieces only, which they reassembled in a way that did no justice to the original. But it was still recognizable; there was just enough to strike a chord with the inner trace left in the soul. Could this account for the sudden spread of Christianity along the same paths, via the same routes that the Hebrews had long ago taken when they spread the Old Myth?

First, Christ himself is depicted as retracing the footsteps of his ancestors, and recapitulating the whole of Hebrew history in a short lifetime: like Joseph he escapes to Egypt; as with Moses, innocent infants are slain; like Joshua, his namesake, he crosses the Jordan near Jericho where he was baptised by John; he then covers the country which his footloose ancestors had conquered, ending up at Jerusalem which was traditionally held by the Jebusites until David's reign. From there, the early Christians carried their new myth to Asia Minor in the wake of the Dannuna, and from there to Greece, Rome and eventually the whole world.

Christ is also presented as the summation of the Old Myth. He was conceived at the Spring Equinox, as were many of the infant gods of the Old Religion, like Horus who was conceived at the Sacred Wedding in the spring. His mother Isis

209

is associated with Virgo, and Mary celebrates her birthday in Virgo to this day. Christ's birth was associated with a well-known cave sacred to Adonis in Bethlehem. John the Baptist, on the other hand, was conceived at the Autumn Equinox and born at the Summer Solstice; it is stated that after his birth his light can only grow less, while the light of Christ will increase. With his four evangelists and their images from the zodiac in the Age of Taurus, and his twelve apostles, he fulfills the requirements of the old myth. He furthermore sends out seventy-two disciples representing all the seventy-two 'pentads' of the zodiac, and seventy-two remained for a long time the traditional number of cardinals around the Pope of Rome.

For many centuries the cycle of the year has been celebrated with many fragments of the old myth still included, such as Psalm 104 which was also read or chanted in the time of the Pharaoh Akhenaten. Could this have been part of his heritage from the Hebrew-speaking foreign rulers before him?

There is no such thing as a new myth. There are only better or worse outward images of what is indelibly inscribed on the inward soul. But we can learn to look at the old myth in a new light. We are beginning to see it in a much more psychological way. And we are learning to value the unconscious dark side of the myth, which is preserved even in such material as nursery rhymes and fairy tales, and expressed spontaneously even in comics and films. Half a myth is inadequate. Only the myth which truly reflects the soul by presenting the complete balanced picture, can help to balance the soul and bring harmony to society.

This is not achieved by piling up facts, however authentic. The soul has a natural shorthand of its own, rediscovered by Freud in the extraordinary compression of dreams. It strips away all the irrelevant facts to reveal the myth. It presses and distils experience into powerful images. One of the hallmarks of myth is that it contains no more than can be celebrated within the cycle of a single year. It is enough.

According to Christian tradition itself, the Age of Christ would last 2,000 years – in other words, coinciding with the Age of Pisces.

So the beginning of the Age of Aquarius will mark the end of the Age of Christ. To be followed by the Age of the Holy Ghost. A more 'ghostly' age which will be more spiritual, more soulful and above all more psychological? Perhaps in this coming age of wisdom, more people will attend to the deep roots of their religions and, at the same time, take care of the inner soul, and the soulwork of reintegrating the superficial ego with its deep unconscious roots. And from these rich sources restore a myth that could accommodate the special individual parts, rather than exclude – not so much unique, as universal.

January, 1990.
St. Ailred's Day.

CHAPTER NOTES

Chapter 1
1 Bright, 1960, p 343
2 *Penguin Dictionary of Archaeology*, 1982, p 118

Chapter 2
1 Budge, 1912, pp 121-41
2 *Genesis* 41.1-8; 41.25-43
3 *Genesis* 13.10

Chapter 3
1 *Exodus* 1.6-8
2 Budge, 1912, pp 93-115
3 *Exodus* 1.7-16; 22; 2.11-12, 23; 3.7, 20-22; 5.1-2, 5-6, 9-11; 6.30; 7.15-18, 20-24; 8.1, 2, 6; 9.3, 6, 7, 8, 9, 10, 13-19, 23-25; 10.7, 13, 14, 15, 21-23; 11.1, 4-6; 12.29-30, 33-38, 1, 2, 6, 8, 9, 14; 13, 3-5, 10
4 Lewis, 1980, pp 24-7
5 *Exodus* 2.1-10
6 Lewis, 1980, pp 28-9
7 *Exodus* 24.4
8 Anati, 1986, pp 290-1
9 Winton Thomas, 1958, p 160
   Erman, 1927, pp. 60-78
10 Prof Cohen, article, 1983, pp 18-29
11 *Numbers* 16.31-4
12 *Numbers* 13.27-8, 33
13 *Joshua* 6.17, 20, 21, 24
14 *Joshua* 4.19-6.20
15 *Joshua* 8.28

Interim Section 2
1 *Kings* 6.1

Chapter 4
1 Gardiner 1961, pp 155-6
    Flavius Josephus, 1841, pp 789-90
2 Gunn and Gardiner, 1918, p 49
3 Gunn and Gardiner, 1918, p 52
4 *Isaiah* 20.16-18, 22-24
5 Kenyon, 1960, p 183
6 *1 Chronicles* 18.3-8
7 *1 Samuel* 18.1-7; 20.35-42
8 *1 Samuel* 31.4
9 *2 Samuel* 1.19, 22
10 *1 Kings* 10.27, 11-12, 14-15, 18-25
11 *1 Kings* 10.28-9
12 Pritchard, 1950, pp 143-9
13 *2 Samuel* 5.3, 7, 8, 9, 11, 12, 13; 7.4, 9, 12, 14, 15, 17, 19,
    28; 8.10, 11; 11.1-5, 14-18, 21, 26, 27; 12.1, 14, 15, 16,
    18, 19, 20, 22, 23, 24, 25, 26-8; 13.6, 10, 11, 14, 22, 23,
    28, 30, 31, 32; 14.24; 15.1, 2, 3, 4, 6, 7, 9, 10, 12; 18.1,
    6, 7, 9, 14, 17, 18, 33; 21.1, 8, 9, 10, 12, 14; *1 Kings*
    1.1-4, 15, 20, 29, 30; 2.10-12; *Psalms* 89.36-7, 29-30
14 Gardiner, 1961, p 163
15 Pritchard, 1950, pp 133-4
16 *1 Kings* 5.7-9; 6.22, 30, 38; 8.5, 12-13, 63, 65
17 Pritchard, 1950, p 132
18 *1 Kings* 10.18-21
19 *1 Kings* 7.48-50, 15, 23, 27-8
20 *2 Chronicles* 12.2-4, 9
21 *Isaiah* 13.17-22
22 *Deuteronomy* 28.59-68
23 *2 Chronicles* 12.7-8
24 Mercer, 1939 (6 extracts), pp 707-17, 249, 255-7, 271-7
25 *1 Kings* 11.19-25
26 *1 Kings* 11.29-32, 36
27 *2 Chronicles* 14.7-8; 15.2-7; 16.2-4

Interim Section 3
1 Gardiner, 1961, p 171
2 Homer, *The Odyssey*, Book XIV, p 226
3 *2 Chronicles* 16.9
4 *Deuteronomy* 28.49-57

Chapter 5
1 *2 Kings* 22.8, 10-13; 23.1-6, 11-14, 20-22
2 *2 Kings* 18.4
3 *2 Kings* 23.24
4 *Jeremiah* 31.31, 32; 27.9; 23.26-27, 32; 44.15-19
5 *Isaiah* 13.4
6 *Jeremiah* 22.6, 7
7 *Isaiah* 21.9; *Ezekiel* 39.2, 6; *Isaiah* 13.4-5, 15-16; *Ezekiel* 38.3-5

SELECT BIBLIOGRAPHY AND FURTHER READING

Aharoni, Y., *The Land of the Bible: A Historical Geography*, 1966, Eng. Trans. 1967 (London: Burns and Oates, Philadelphia: Westminster Press)

Like the Hebrews, but a thousand years earlier, the Hebrew-speaking West Semites lived in the Negeb before invading the Levant, where Palestine-Syria were a single unit in the Middle Bronze Age. The author suggests certain traditions have been preserved in the Bible from this early period: Early Bronze Age irrigation works (*Gen* 13.10) and Hazor as greatest of cities (*Josh* 11.10). Lists the Hyksos fortress towns, and suggests horse-drawn chariotry brought with it a feudal structure, as later in Solomon's time. Seti I seems to claim succession to Hyksos rulers.

Albright, William Foxwell, *The Israelite Conquest of Canaan in the Light of Archaeology*, 1939. Bulletin of the American Schools of Oriental Research, 74

The Hebrew account of the destruction of Ai 'reflects a much older West Semite tradition with regard to the fall of the Early Bronze Age city'. (p 17)

Anati, Emmanuel, *Palestine before the Hebrews*, 1963 (London: Jonathan Cape)

Anati, E., *The Mountain of God*, 1986 (New York: Rizzoli International)

A landmark in redating the Hebrew Chronicle. At Har Karkom, Anati finds temple and standing stones that correspond to descriptions of Mount Sinai. He concludes the Exodus took place 1,000 years earlier than previously supposed, and he gives credit to several scholars who have pointed out the parallels between the Admonitions of Ipuwer and the Biblical account of the plagues. He suggests the identification of the Habiru with the Hebrews and of Sargon with Moses.

Astour, Michael, *Hellenosemitica: An ethnic and cultural study in West Semitic impact on Mycenean Greece*, 1965 (Leidon: E. J. Brill)

Barker, Margaret, *The Older Testament: The Survival of themes from the ancient royal cult in sectarian Judaism and Christianity*, 1987 (London: SPCK)

Barton, George Aaron, *Semitic and Hamitic Origins, social and religious*, 1934 (Philadelphia: University of Pennsylvania Press)

Semites dominate the majority of provinces in Lower Egypt (the Delta) during the Old Kingdom. Compares the Ark of Amun with the Ark of Yahweh.

✓ Bermant, Chaim, and Weitzman, Michael, *Ebla: an archaeological enigma*, 1978 (London: Book Club Associates)

Possible mention of Abraham, Moses, Israel, as well as Sodom and Gomorrah and the other cities of the plain, but from a library dated *c.* 2300 BC – a thousand years too early. This is the enigma.

Blavatsky, Helena, *Isis*, 1877 (New York. Reprinted Theosophical Society Publications)

Blavatsky, H., *The Secret Doctrine*, 1888 (London. Reprinted Theosophical Society Publications)

In the field of comparative religion she anticipated much of what we now take for granted – with considerable learning to support it. She also suggested that the pyramids were made of cement, deduced from an ancient picture of a man climbing a half-finished pyramid with a bag of sand (cp. Davidovitz).

Bright, John, *A History of Israel*, 1960 (London: SCM Press)

His concise prologue and first chapter are informative for the Age of Myth. A clear exposition of the currently accepted late dating follows, with useful maps and chronological charts at the back.

Bronner, Leah, *The Stories of Elijah and Elisha as Polemics Against Baal Worship*, 1968 (Leiden: E. J. Brill)

Budge, Sir Ernest Alfred Wallis, *The Book of the Dead*, 1899 (London: Kegan Paul, revised 1923, Arkana 1985)

Especially for illustrations related to zodiac, facing p 388, and p 620.

Budge, Sir E. A. W., *An account of the coffin of Seti I, King of Egypt BC 1370*, 1908 (Trustees, Sir John Soane's Museum)

This coffin text, also known as the *Book of Gates*, seems to contain vestiges of the twelve celestial mansions of the zodiac.

Budge, Sir E. A. W., *Egyptian Literature*, 1912 (London: Kegan Paul)

Volume I: The Legends of the Gods, Chapter 2 (pp. 121–141) for the introduction, text and translation of the story of Imhotep and the seven year famine. The text is late Ptolemaic (Third Century BC) but is thought to be a copy of an older document (cp. Hurry).

Budge, Sir E. A. W., *From Fetish to God in Ancient Egypt*, 1935 (London: Oxford University Press)

A masterpiece on Egyptian religion with fascinating illustrations.

Clay, Albert Tobias, *The Empire of the Amorites*, 1919 (Newhaven: Yale Oriental Series)

From available materials constructs a picture of West Semite power from before the arrival of the Sumerians to the collapse of Hammurabi's Empire. Argues for the Semitic origin of writing – which the Sumerians then monopolized. Suggests West Semites from the Lebanon Mountains built the ziggurats and pyramids.

Cohane, John Philip, *The Key*, 1969 (Turnstone Press)

Mostly from place names, divine names, etc. reconstructs a picture of Northwest Semites travelling worldwide and spreading their culture during the Age of Myth and before. He has pointed the way to a fascinating new branch of etymology.

Cohen, Rudolph, 'The Mysterious MBI People', 1983 (*Biblical Archaeology Review*, Vol IX, 4)

His investigation of the Negeb reveals a concentration of sites dating from the Middle Bronze Age (*c.* 2200 BC) especially East of Kadesh Barnea which recall the Israelite tradition of camping near this oasis (*Deut* 1.46). He cannot rule out the possible identification of this MBI people, who appear to have come out of Egypt (with ground Aswan granite and ostrich eggshells) on their way to attack and destroy the fortified cities of Jericho and Ai, with the Israelites and their famed Exodus.

Cohen, R., *First International Conference on Biblical Archaeology*, 1984

His finds show evidence that the Israelite Exodus took place a thousand years earlier than the accepted dating.

Critchlow, Keith, *Time Stands Still: new light on megalithic science*, 1979 (London: Gordon Fraser)

Applies Thom's findings to sites on Bodmin Moor. Suggests the builders used Pythagorean mathematics a thousand years before Pythagoras and may have been literate.

Cross, Frank More, *Canaanite Myth and Hebrew Epic: Essays*

on the history of the religion of Israel, 1974 (Harvard University Press)

Parallels between old Semite and Hebrew religion, for example, 'El Olam' (Lord of Eternity) already in use at the time of Sargon.

Danielou, Alain, *Shiva and Dionysus. The Religion of Nature and Eros*, 1979 (France: Librarie Arthème Fayard, 1984. Trans. K. F. Hurry. New York: Inner Traditions International)

Traces the link between Shiva and the Tamil-speaking Dravidians in India; the Sumerians; the cult of Osiris in Egypt; and Dionysos in Greece.

Davidovitz, Joseph, *Book of Stone. Alchemy in the Pyramids, Vol I*, 1984 (Detroit: Applied Archaeological Sciences, Geo-Polymer Institute)

Desborough, Vincent Robert d'Arba, *The Greek Dark Ages. The end of the Mycenean Civilization and the Dark Age. The archaeological background*, 1962 (Cambridge University Press)

Significantly, Greek historians such as Hesiod, Herodotus, Thucydides, appear to have known nothing of this Dark Age, although it lasted several centuries.

Doane, T. W., *Bible Myths and their Parallels in Other Religions*, 1882 (New York: Commonwealth Co)

A valuable, neglected book, which (along with Blavatsky, Frazer, etc.), in the nineteenth century, was already forcing the reader towards the (then) unpopular conclusion that the many existing religions derived from a single source.

Drummond, Sir William, *Oedipus Judaicus*, 1811 (Privately printed, 1986. Rilko Books)

Assesses place of zodiac in Hebrew tradition.

✓   Edwards, I. E. S., *The Pyramids of Egypt*, 1947 (Penguin Books)

The first step-pyramid orientated North suggests an astral cult.

Erman, Adolph (Trans.), *The Literature of the Ancient Egyptians: poems, narratives and manuals of instruction*, Eng. Trans. A. M. Blackman, 1927 (London: Methuen)

Includes Admonitions of Ipuwer and Nefferrohu (see Ipuwer). The Instructions of Ptah-hotep and Merikare, from the Old Kingdom, are in apodictic as well casuistic form, like the commands of Moses. For example, Do not kill, Do not be covetous. Or, He who honours his father, the memory of him remains in the mouth of the living. Includes the Tale of Sinuhe, who lived in exile in the Levant during the Middle Kingdom.

Foucart, George B., *Calendars (Egyptian) Encyclopedia of Religion and Ethics*, Ed. James Hastings, 1910 (Edinburgh: Clarke)
Thinks that the annual inundation of the Nile coinciding with the reappearance of Sirius in the night sky, may have led to the cult of the heavens – a major step for religion. Also suggests that the cult of the zodiac is much older than supposed, but the evidence, which would naturally be on the ceilings of the temples, has been destroyed.

✓ Frazer, Sir James George, *The Golden Bough: A study in magic and religion*, 1890–1915. Abridged Edition 1924 (London: Macmillan)
For copious parallels between myths, especially on the Adonis type.

✓ Gardiner, Sir Alan, *Egypt of the Pharaohs*, 1961 (Oxford: Clarendon Press)
For the much debated historicity of the Imhotep inscription, which at the very least has preserved accurately the names of King Netjrikhe Djöser, see p 76. For a convincing background for the Joseph stories in the Old Kingdom see p 91ff. Where the tomb-owner inspects bakers, brewers etc. and Weni, a man of humble birth, becomes a high official. For Apophis' temple of fair and everlasting beauty see p 163 (see also Gunn)

✓ Gaster, Theodor Herzl, *Thespis: Ritual, Myth and Drama in the Ancient Near East*, 1950 (New York: Henry Schuman)
A brilliant reconstruction of the development of Greek drama from Semite myth and Egyptian ritual. Gaster suggests the dismemberment of Tammuz underlies Greek tragedy and more particularly the *Bow of Aqhat* as the earlier version of *Philoctetes's Bow* by Sophocles. Many striking parallels between Bronze Age Semite rituals and Hebrew tradition: the monster Tannin, the battle of light and dark, the fall of the Gods (p 82) are all based on ancient Semite myth. Like other Bronze Age Temples, Solomon's Temple (*1 Kgs* 8.12) was orientated on the Equinox (see Keret)

Ginsberg, H. L., (Trans.) (see Keret)

Gleadow, Rupert, *The Origins of the Zodiac*, 1968 (London: Cape)
From classical times only.

Glover, Terrot Reaveley, *The Ancient World*, 1944 (London: Pelican)
Amber from the Baltic and jade from China in the Near East of the Bronze Age.

Glueck, Nelson, *Rivers in the Desert: The exploration of the Negev*, 1959 (London: Weidenfeld and Nicholson)
A freak occupation of the Negev – otherwise uninhabited for centuries – which lasted only a few decades. (cp. Cohen who has re-examined these same traces.)

Goldziher, Ignacz, *Myth Among the Hebrews and its Historic Development*, 1877, Trans. R. Martineau (London)

Gordon, Cyrus H., *Ugarit as link between Greek and Hebrew Literatures*, 1954 (Rome: Rivesta Degli Studi Orientali)
Compares the epic ballad form in the Ugarit literature, in the Bible and in Homer, and specifically compares Keret's abduction of his wife, Hurriya, from Pabel, with David retrieving Mickal from Paltiel (*2 Sam* 3.15). Also compares warrior women and ageless women from both literatures.

Gordon, C. H. 'Minoan Linear A', 1958, *Journal of Near Eastern Studies 17*

Gordon, C. H., *Before the Bible: The common background of Greek and Hebrew civilization*, 1962 (London: Collins)
Cites bull-grappling as evidence of a common culture that once united the Eastern Mediterranean from Agade to Crete. Notes biblical names at Ugarit: Abram or Abiram, Ysrael, Moses and Puah; and the Ugarit god Mot honoured in the name of one of David's mighty men. Compares famine as punishment for sin in the reign of Keret and David; Baal's temple with Solomon's temple; the Bull El, father of seventy gods with the Bull of Jacob, with his seventy offspring (*Ex* 1.5). Mycenean and Phoenician sagas find parallels in Samson, and he finds an ancient Bronze Age core to the Book of Job. Supports Kaufman's conviction that the 'Priestly (P)' sections of the Bible are much older than the Babylonian exile.

Gordon, C. H., *The Mediterranean Factor in the Old Testament*, 1963 (Leiden: Supplement to *Vetus Testamentum*, 9)
In the Bronze Age the name of Dan is common, Issacher is mentioned in Minoan texts from Crete, where there was found the inscription, 'Dawida is chief'.

Gordon, C. H., *Before Columbus: Links between the Old World and Ancient America*, 1972 (London: Turnstone Press)

Gray, John, *The Legacy of Canaan. The Ras Shamra Texts and their relevance to the Old Testament*, 1957 (Leiden: E.J. Brill)

Gray, John, *Archaeology and the Old Testament World*, 1962 (London: Thomas Nelson)

Gray, John, *The Canaanites*, 1964 (London: Thames and Hudson)

He refers to the 'astonishing similarity' between the Bronze Age Semites in the Levant and the Hebrews, pointing out many specific parallels in their language, writing, architecture and way of life. Cosmetics, golden bangles, golden mice, burial customs, ritual seclusion after childbirth, etc., are all compared, as well as the change from tribal to feudal organization. Outlines clearly the development of writing, i.e. of the proto-Hebrew alphabet and script in the Bronze Age. Has no doubt about the literary achievement of these West Semites, though little has survived. Other comparisons include gargantuan feasts to dedicate a temple, incubation dreams at Gubna as at Gibeon, laws, liturgy and taxation systems, which included levies of silver, produce or labour in both cases. Passages from the El-Amarna letters also occur in the Psalms and Prophets. (See also Keret Legend.)

Greenberg, Moshe, *The Hap/biru*, 1955, American Oriental Series, Vol 39 (New Haven: Yale University Press)

Collected texts about the Habiru (etymologically identical with Hebrews), who appear first in the Old Kingdom of Egypt and not after the twelfth century BC. (cp. Mendenhall for their role in the El-Amarna period)

Gunn, Battiscombe, and Gardiner, Alan H., 'The Expulsion of the Hyksos', 1918, *Journal of Egyptian Archaeology*, V

First hand confirmation that the Hyksos (foreign rulers) introduced horses. Gives reasons for early speculations about the vast empire of these invaders, and includes the tomb inscription of Ahmose which provides a personal eye-witness account of the fall of Avaris, the spoil taken from it; the three-year siege of Sharuren; and a later expedition to Mesopotamia.

Hallo, William, 'A Sumerian Amphictyony', 1963, *Journal of Cuneiform Studies* XIV, p 88

The Third Dynasty of Ur provides evidence of typical Hebrew tribal, amphictyony: the city states served the central shrine at Nippur in a monthly rotation. (cp. *1 Kings* 4.7). Hallo thinks the Sumerians adapted their system from an earlier older tribal system.

Harrison, Jane, *Prolegomena to the study of Greek Religion*, 1903, Cambridge, 1962 (London: Merlin)

Harrison, Richard J., *The Beaker Folk: Copper Age Archaeology in Western Europe*, 1980 (London: Thames and Hudson)

Hart, George, *Dictionary of Egyptian Gods and Goddesses*, 1986 (London: Routledge Kegan Paul)

Particularly interesting on the Semite God Yah.

Hawkes, Jessie Jacquetta, *The First Great Civilizations: life in Mesopotamia, the Indus Valley and Egypt*, 1973 (London: Hutchinson)

The proto-literate leaders in Mesopotamia were bearded with long hair in the Semite fashion, and their elegant painted pottery was replaced by Sumerian plain ware. Treats the relations between Mesopotamia and the Indus Valley.

Heyerdahl, Thor, *Kon-tiki*, 1951 (London: Allen and Unwin)

✓   Homer, *The Odyssey*, Trans. E. V. Rieu, 1946 (London: Penguin)

Book XIV (p 226) for account of expedition to Egypt.

✓   Hooke, S. H., *Middle Eastern Mythology*, 1963 (London: Penguin)

A mythological substratum in Hebrew tradition up to the time of Elijah and Elisha – closely related to Mesopotamian and Canaanite myth.

Hurry, Jamieson B., *Imhotep, the Vizier and Physician of King Zozer, and afterwards the Egyptian God of Medicine*, 1926 (Oxford) 1978 (Chicago: Ares)

Compares Imhotep's responsibilities as Vizier with Joseph's jurisdiction (p 5) and notes similarity between the Legend of the Seven Year Famine and *Genesis* 41.54f. The author accepts the findings of Sethe (*Imhotep der Asklepios der Aegypter*, 1902, p 11) and Budge, and thinks the legend in its earlier form may be as old as the Third Dynasty; in contrast with G. Maspero's view that the legend was a fabrication (*The Dawn of Civilization*, 1894, p 240).

Ipuwer, The Admonitions of, twenty-third century BC. Redrafted sixteenth century BC. Trans. Erman, 1927

In the first poem (pp 94–100) each verse opens, 'Nay but . . .'; the second poem (pp 100–103) each verse opens, 'Behold . . .' the surviving fragments from the third to sixth poems (pp 104–108) open respectively 'Destroyed . . .', 'Destroy . . .', 'Remember . . .' and 'It is good . . .'. I have selected and rearranged the verses from these poems to bring out the parallels with the Hebrew account of the Plagues. Seters would place the Admonitions in the second intermediate period, but his arguments are purely on linguistic grounds, and suggest the language was revised: but the events themselves refer to the collapse of the Old Kingdom, the view of the majority of Egyptologists in the last few decades.

Jack, J. W., *The Ras Shamra Tablets: their bearing on the Old Testament*, 1935 (Edinburgh: T. & T. Clarke)
Many parallels in the cult of the North West Semites in the Bronze Age and the Hebrews: they celebrated identical feasts that lasted seven days, and both celebrated the feast of unleavened bread; identical sacrifices including peace, sin and trespass offerings; and used the same cult words for Holy of Holies, Table of God, the ephod and the teraphim. Elohim (The Gods) is Lord of the Habiru at Ugarit, as he is Lord of the Northern Hebrew tribes. The name of the Hyksos ruler Khyan is Ahian in the Bible. Ugarit trades with Ophir in the Bronze Age.
Jastrow, Morris, *A Fragment of the Babylonian Dibarra Epic*, 1891 (Pennsylvania: University Press)
Jastrow, M., *The Religion of Babylonia and Assyria*, 1898 (Boston: Ginn)
See Ch 22 especially for astrology, sacred numbers, and the way maths derives ultimately from religion.
Jayne, W. A., *The Healing Gods of Ancient Civilizations*, 1925 (New Haven: Yale)
Jaynes, Julian, *The Origins of Consciousness in the breakdown of the bicameral mind*, 1982 (Houghton Mifflin)
Josephus, Flavius, *The Works of the Learned and authentic Jewish Historian*, first century AD. Trans. William Whiston, 1841 (London: Orlando Hodgson) Trans. Thackeray, H. St. J., 1926 (London: Putnam)
See *Against Apion*, Book 1/14–16, 26–31, for extant passages from Manetho, the Egyptian historian, on the Hyksos, including Apap.
Kaufmann, Yehezkel, *The Religion of Israel, from its Beginnings to the Babylonian Exile*, Abbr. Eng. Trans. 1960 (Chicago: University Press)
Kenyon, Kathleen Mary, *Digging Up Jericho*, 1957 (London: Ernest Benn)
See especially Ch. 8, 'Nomadic Invaders', whose point of entry was Jericho, where the massive wall, thick as the previous triple wall in one, and made with extra large bricks on stone foundations, fell outwards in yet another earthquake. The newcomers were plainly religious from the way they disposed of their dead in nearby tombs.
Kenyon, K. M., *Archaeology in the Holy Land*, 1960 (London: Ernest Benn)

Does not minimize the difficulties of reconciling the archaeological evidence with the Biblical account (within the accepted chronological structure). In the archaeological evidence, she can find 'no trace' of any conquest. And she finds only abject poverty in the time allocated to Solomon, not one recognizably imported object (p 256) and no mining activity at Arabah (p 346). The Millo around Jerusalem is too early for Solomon (LB), and his building activities outside Jerusalem appear negligible. By contrast, every city so far investigated, including Jericho and Ai, was burned by the invaders at the end of the Early Bronze Age and the Hyksos were responsible for truly monumental cities. 'The ethnic ingredients of the Hyksos accords well with what we know about the Habiru.'

Kenyon, K. M., *Amorites and Canaanites*, 1966 (Oxford: University Press)

Distinguishes between the Semites on the coastal plain ('Canaanites') and the West Semites ('Amorites') inland in the hills. There was an exceptionally thick layer of ash at Gubna marking its destruction at the end of the EB period, but she suggests the new settled culture, after the period of hiatus (her EB/MB), stemmed from there.

Kenyon, K. M., *Digging up Jerusalem*, 1974 (London: E. Benn)

Some work on the shaft to the spring of Gihon in the eighteenth century BC, but the city did not reach prominence till LB, when there were huge stone structures and stone-filled terraces (the Millo).

Keret, The Legend of King, Fifteenth Century BC. Trans. Ginsberg, H.L., in Pritchard, James B., *Ancient Near Eastern Texts*, 1950 (Princeton: University Press) pp 142–155

For variant readings, which come closer to the Hebrew account of David's career in some instances, see:

Fr. trans. Charles Virolleaud, *La Legende de Keret*, 1936 (Paris: Biblioteque Archaeologique et Historique)

For possible mention of men from Asher and Zebulun among Keret's troops.

Trans. Gaster, T.H., *The Oldest Stories in the World*, 1960 (Viking)

Trans. Gray, John, 1955 (Leiden: E. H. Brill) (cp Winton Thomas)

Kramer, S. N., *Sumerian Mythology*, 1961 (Pennsylvania: University Press)

Contains an illustration of a seal with seven figures that relate to the zodiac.

Langdon, Stephen Herbert, *Tammuz and Ishtar*, 1914 (Oxford: Clarendon Press)

Suggests the Biblical use of 'Adonai' originally referred to Tammuz. Points out that the Israelites always worshipped the Queen of Heaven and made cakes in her honour (*Jeremiah* 7.18, 44.17). The six-pointed star was the West Semite symbol of the goddess.

Langdon, S. H., *Babylonian Menologies and the Semitic Calendars*, 1933 (Schweich Lectures, 1935 (Oxford: University Press)

Like Gordon and Kaufmann, he traces Mesopotamian influence on the Hebrews to long before the Exile (and doubts that the detested 2nd Babylon would have left much impression). Suggests the influence dates from the time of Hammurabi when, for example, the firstborn of the flocks were offered around 14th Nisan (Passover) and libations were poured out (as at the Feast of Tents). Northwest Semites and Hebrews shared the same Hag Asiph (Ingathering) Festival, and used the same month names till Solomon's reign: Abib (*Deut* 16.1), Ziv (*1 Kgs* 6.1), Bul (*1 Kgs* 6.38) and Etamin (*1 Kgs* 8.2). Associates monthly feasts and their myths with the zodiac, and compares Hebrew tribes with the signs.

Langdon, S. H., *Semitic Mythology*, 1936 *Mythology of all races, Vol V* (Boston: Marshall Jones, for the Archaeological Institute of America)

Like Budge (1935), identifies Marduk's title 'Asari' with Osiris. Finds parallels between Gilgamesh and Samson.

Larousse Encyclopaedia of Mythology, Trans. Aldington and Ames, 1959 (London: Batchworth)

Lewis, Brian, *The Sargon Legend. A study of the Akkadian text, and the tale of the hero who was exposed at birth*, 1980 (Cambridge, Mass.: American School of Oriental Research, dissertation series, 4)

Compares the birth of Sargon with that of Moses and Horus in Egypt. Plus the fragmentary account of Sargon in the wilderness.

Lockyer, Joseph Norman, *The Dawn of Astronomy. A study in the Temple Worship and Mythology of Ancient Egypt*, 1964 (Cambridge, Mass: MIT Paperback)

Mackenzie, Donald A., *Egyptian Myth and Legend*, 1924 (London: Gresham)

Matthiae, Paolo, *Ebla: an Empire Rediscovered*, 1980 (London: Hodder) Compare Bermant.

Maunder, E. W. and Maunder, A.S.D.R., *The Oldest Astronomy*, 1908 (Journal of the British Astronomical Assn, 14)

Meek, T. J., *Hebrew Origins*, 1933 Haskell Lectures, 1934 (New York and London: Harper)

A study of polytheism and henotheism within the Hebrew tradition. Traces the Bull Cult to the rival priesthood of Aaron from before the conquest. Detects the Tammuz cult in Solomon's Song (cp W. H. Schoff, *A Symposium*, 1924, Philadelphia)

Mendenhall, G. E., *The Tenth Generation*, 1973 (Baltimore and London: Johns Hopkins University Press)

Discerns that the Habiru, in the El-Amarna letters, are the native population throwing off the imperial rule of Egypt. The letters tell a story of internal power struggle, conspiracy and revolt (p 126ff). With Egypt weak, the Habiru regained increasing control over their own country.

Mercer, Samuel A. B., (Trans.) *The Tell El-Amarna Tablets*, (2 Vols) 1939 (Toronto: Macmillan)

Complete letters in English, plus concise appendix on the Habiru.

Neferrohu, (see Erman, pp 111–114)

Olmstead, Albert Ten Eyck, *History of Palestine and Syria*, 1931 (New York and London: C. Scribner's Sons)

Sacred trees, like the oak at Mamre, circles of stones, ancient rites at the Spring Equinox, as well as the specific sacred sites at Bethel, were the centres of cult from prehistoric times. Compares Phoenician with Biblical cosmology. Traces the relationship between Old Akkadian and Old Egyptian languages. Points out the prominence of Seth (the West Semite Baal Saphon) in the Old Kingdom of Egypt and again in the Hyksos period. The splendour of Egypt's New Empire owed much to Canaan. The Bronze Age Semites 'anticipate Hebrew usage and Biblical style'.

Patai, Raphael, *The Hebrew Goddess*, 1967 (New York: Ktav)

Compares the gods and rituals of the Old Semites with those of the Hebrews and thinks that Israel worshipped the ancient Canaanite gods and goddesses almost throughout their history. This polytheism was suppressed for a short time only, and re-emerged in the Apocalyptic writing. Patai finds a parallel of the Tetragrammaton in the Egyptian Shu-Tefnut-Geb-Nut. The reformed cult of Yahweh could absorb the gods but not the ancient Goddess, worshipped from 4000 BC: the Virgin Harlot of War and Love.

Patton, J. H., *Canaanite Parallels to the Book of Psalms*, 1944 (Baltimore: Johns Hopkins)
From this detailed study, concludes that Ugaritic literature and the Psalms appear to be contemporary works.

Penguin Dictionary of Archaeology, ed. Warwick Bray and David Trump, 1970 (London: Penguin)

Pritchard, James B. (ed.) *Ancient Near Eastern Texts: relating to the Old Testament*, 1950 (Princeton: University Press)
Valuable collection of original sources. For the gilded throne p 132, and the Temple and Palace pp 133–134. Cp. Keret.

Ringgren, Helmer, *Israelite Religion*, Trans. David Green, 1966 (London: SPCK)

Ringgren, H., *Religions of the Ancient Near East*, Trans. John Sturdy, 1973 (London: SPCK)

Rogers, Robert William, *Cuneiform Parallels with the Old Testament*, 1912 (London: Henry Froude)

van Seters, J., *The Hyksos: A new investigation*, 1967 (New Haven)
Excellent reassessment of the magnificence of the Hyksos period – in stark contrast with Manetho's dark account. Monumental architecture of palaces, temples, and great city gates at Hazor and Megiddo. Paved streets and covered drains at Shechem. A period of diplomatic alliances cemented by marriage contracts. A particular design of stone jar used by the Hyksos, suggests their origins were in Syria, that they were in Egypt in the Pyramid Age, were rulers of the Levant in the Middle Bronze Age, from there conquered Egypt, and continued in the Levant in the Late Bronze Age.

Shapiro, Max S. and Hendricks, Rhoda A., *A Dictionary of Mythologies*, 1981 (London: Granada)

Stancioff, Marion Mitchell, *Files*, Work still in progress 1933–1990.
To be housed at Warburg, London. Perhaps the most comprehensive collection of symbols in existence amassed on file cards in the course of more than half a century, with full bibliography. Includes a valuable collection of cards on the cult of the zodiac throughout the ages, as well as the particular celestial beasts.

Thierens, A. E., *Astrology in Mesopotamian Culture*, 1935 (Leiden: Brill)

Thom, Alexander, *Megalithic Sites in Britain*, 1967 (Oxford: University Press)

Thom, A., *Megalithic Lunar Observatories*, 1971 (Oxford: University Press)

Thom, A. and Thom, A. S., *Megalithic Remains in Britain and Brittany*, 1978 (Oxford: University Press)
Finds evidence of an eight-part calendar. (cp. Critchlow)

Thomas, Winton D., (ed.) *Documents from Old Testament Times*, 1958 (Edinburgh and London: Thomas Nelson)
Includes Hammurabi law code and Biblical parallels; teaching of Amenophis and in comparison with *Proverbs* 22–24; vestiges of the Baal liturgy in, for example, *Psalm* 48.2; and 'the striking correspondence' between the life and characters in Ugaritic Literature and Hebrew Literature, for example 'The Canaanite Absalom'.

✓   de Vaux, Roland, *Ancient Israel*, Trans. John McHugh, 1961 (New York: McGraw-Hill)
Copious examples of Israelite customs originating in an earlier period. Compares the lamb substituted for the infant in old Phoenician and Hebrew Cult, notes the continuity of burial customs from the Bronze Age through to the Israelite period. Links the Apocalyptic Book of Jubilees with ancient Canaanite cult. And compares Solomon's palace and temple with the Hyksos complex at Hazor.

de Vaux, R., 'Le problème des Hapiru après Quinze Années', 1968, *Journal of Near Eastern Studies*, 27, p 221 (Chicago: University Press)
Suggests the 'Habiru' could be a race, and not a lowly class.

Vawter, B., 'The Canaanite Background of *Genesis* 49', 1955, *Catholic Biblical Quarterly*, 17, p 13ff.
One of the most archaic passages of Hebrew verse in the Bible invokes the Ugaritic deities.

Velikovsky, Immanuel, *Ages in Chaos, Volume I: A reconstruction of ancient history from the Exodus to King Akhnaton*, 1952 (London: Sidgwick and Jackson)
His greatest contribution has been to question the chronology of the Bible in relation to the rest of the Ancient Near East. In particular, he notices the parallels between: the Admonitions of Ipuwer and the account of the Plagues; the booty depicted on walls of Karnac (Luxor) and the furnishings of Solomon's Temple; and correspondences between the El Amarna letters and the period following the collapse of Solomon's Empire in the Hebrew Chronicle, especially the undoubtedly ancient names of Jehosaphat's colonels (*2 Chron* 17.14–20)

Webster, James Carson, *The Labours of the Months*, 1938 (Evaston and Chicago: Northwestern University Studies in the Humanities, 4)
Celestial mansions of the gods are reduced to the heroic exploits of men and linger on as monthly tasks of a comparatively banal nature.

Woolley, Sir Leonard, *Ur of the Chaldees*, 1929 (London: Pelican Books)
'Mes-kalam-dug' p 57ff.

✓ Woolley, Sir L., *A Forgotten Kingdom*, 1953 (London: Penguin (Pelican) Books)
Imaginative archaeology. Traces the path of civilization from Mesopotamia across Syria to Crete. His findings at the site of ancient Alalakh anticipate the equally remarkable, more recent, finds at nearby Ebla, which tend to confirm Woolley's deductions.

Index to Bible

Relevant Proper Names, Subjects and Key Words
The Holy Bible Revised Standard Version Catholic Edition, Trans. from original tongues AD 1611. Revised 1885 and 1952. Catholic Truth Society, London.